YOGA

THE CLASSICAL WAY

BY

SRI INDAR NATH

ISBN 1 872255 00 0

First Edition 1989 1000 copies
Second Edition 1992 1000 copies
Third Edition 2001 1000 copies

Illustrations by Sharon White and Joanna Novy
Photographs by Sydney Orleans Harding

Published by Jane Sill, Tower White
FOR THE PATANJALI YOGA CENTRE

Printed in England by The Print Station, Hastings TN34 3TY

DEDICATION

This book is dedicated to Puja Ma Yogashakti,
who first inspired me to follow the path of
classical Yoga and to my dear wife,
Sudharma, who helped me
to continue my journey on this path.

*May it help the seekers after
Truth to find their way to Self
Realisation.*

Maharishi Patanjali   (*Line drawing by Joanna Novy*)

CONTENTS

LIST OF ILLUSTRATIONS

Page

ACKNOWLEDGEMENTS

I would like to render my sincere thanks to those who have helped me publish this book.

First of all, I am greatly indebted to Brian Netscher, at that time editor 'Yoga Today', who approached me to write a few articles for the magazine which paved the way for the book. Secondly my grateful thanks go to the following people: Elizabeth Fennel, at that time Secretary to the Centre, who had the hard task of researching and compiling the material; to Avril Kirk for typing the first script and Dennis Benton for his valuable suggestions; to Dr. Vamberto Morais, himself a writer and broadcaster, for his valuable advice and foreward to this book. My grateful thanks go to Ewa Cobham, ex-Secretary of the Centre for editing the book. Dr. Mari Taber for completing the first computer setting; Jane Sill and Sydney Orleans Harding for the photography. My special thanks go to Sharon White who has skilfully designed the cover and the drawings. May God shower His choicest blessings upon every one of them.

Finally, I prostrate to all Yoga Masters past and present and mentioned herein whose works have inspired me to write this book.

FOREWORD

The present flood of books and manuals on Yoga (most of them on Hatha Yoga and sometimes restricted to the Asanas) is bewildering to the student, particularly to the beginner. With the present book, originally published as a series of articles in 'Yoga Today', one can be sure that it comes right from the original Indian source and is firmly based on the great treatises like the Hatha Yoga Pradipika and the Gheranda Samhita. All those who know Sri Indar Nath and have worked with him are aware not only of his outstanding qualities as teacher and friend, but also of his unfaltering devotion to Yoga and the pains he takes to be faithful to a great tradition.

Vamberto Morais

YOGASRI INDAR NATH

Sri Indar Ji as he is called, was born in Punjab, a State of Northern India in November, 1923. He came to London with his wife and family in 1957 on the staff of the High Commission of India. He later joined the British Post Office and worked at its Headquarters for more than twenty-one years until his retirement in 1983.

Born of a devout Hindu family, his interest in Yoga goes back to childhood, but his deep devotion to classical yoga developed in England.

During his years as Secretary of the Hindu Centre of London, Indar met and entertained many visiting Swamis. In 1967 he met Ma Yogashakti, the first lady Swami to tour abroad. She encouraged him to devote himself to practising and spreading the true message of Yoga. In the following year he derived further inspiration from Swami Satyananda.

Sri Indar's first response was to start a Yoga class at the Hindu Centre and then to set up a Yoga club at the Post Office Headquarters, of which he remained Secretary until his retirement.

In 1972, he founded the Yoga Centre of North London, later to be renamed the Patanjali Yoga Centre to reflect its dedication to traditional Yoga.

Since his retirement, Sri Indar has devoted all his time to the Patanjali Yoga Centre and the cause of Yoga. He has run teachers' training courses for the British Wheel of Yoga and conducts many seminars and retreats for other Yoga groups in this country and abroad. He has also taken classes for the Inner London Education Authority's Evening Institutes. He is a representative for the United Kingdom of the International Yoga Co-ordination Centre, Delhi.

Sri Indar was awarded the title of Yogasri (Lord of Yoga) by Vishwa Yoga Samaj for his services in the field of Yoga. He has been honoured with the title of Vishwa Yoga Ratna (Jewel of the World Wide Yoga) and Yogacharya by the World Development Parliament. He was also elected as Fellow Member of the Indian Society for Clinical-Yoga in 1988.

During his tour of India in 1986, Sri Indar was initiated at the Sivananda Ashram at Rishikesh, Himalayas, by Sri Swami Krishnananda Ji of the Divine Life Society.

INTRODUCTION

" Salutations to Adinatha who expounded
the knowledge of Hatha Yoga, which like
a stair-case, leads the aspirant to the
high-pinnacled Raja Yoga."
(Hatha Yoga Pradipika, Invocation.)

In the Hindu tradition all writings begin with a dedication to the Guru, the Master. For a book on Hatha Yoga, no fitter opening could be found than salutations to the supreme Guru, Adinatha the Lord Siva himself.

The world today is witnessing a phenomenal surge of interest in all forms of Yoga. The demand for teachers far outstrips supply; new Yoga Centres open almost daily and Yoga literature abounds. As Swami Chidananda of Rishikesh once pointed out, the West has produced more books on Yoga during the past twenty years than India produced in the last two hundred.

However, Western interest in Yoga is no mere fleeting whim of our generation. Two hundred years ago Western Sanskrit scholars and translators were at work and visiting Swamis have been coming to the British Isles since early in Queen Victoria's reign. Before the close of the nineteenth century the great Vivekananda had erupted on the West with pungent criticism of the dangers which could come of heeding Eastern *"mystery mongers"* and Western *"so-called teachers"*.

It is not helpful to indulge in any mystery mongering. This survey of Hatha Yoga deals with simple concepts with which many readers may already be familiar.

First, then, for the basic framework:

1

What is Yoga?

The word *"Yoga"*, as most Yoga students know, comes from the Sanskrit verb *"yuj"*, which means to yoke, unite or join.

Swami Sivananda, one of the world's greatest modern Yogis and writers on Yoga, defines the science of Yoga as that which *"teaches us the method of joining the individual soul with the Supreme Soul"*. Others use phrases such as Self Realization, Self Knowledge and the yoking of all the powers of the body, mind and soul to God.

There are many different types of Yoga. No one knows how they evolved, their origins being probably prehistoric. Certainly, the earliest of the Vedic scriptures refer to what was evidently already a strong and ancient tradition.

In the present book we shall concern ourselves with only two of the paths of Yoga: *"Hatha Yoga"* often called the *"Yoga of strength"* and *"Raja Yoga"*, usually translated as *"the royal path of Yoga"*.

Raja Yoga and Hatha Yoga

The earliest known treatise on Raja Yoga is attributed to Patanjali who is said to have been a philosopher, Yogi, logician and physician, living approximately 300-400 years before Christ. His work on codifying and reformulating the existing ancient Yoga philosophy is in the form of *"Sutras"* or aphorisms which were to comprise brief teaching notes for his students to commit to memory and on which they would subsequently base their own teachings.

Patanjali's exposition on Raja Yoga is a complete philosophy of healthy, ethical, moral and spiritual living. There are eight steps on the *"staircase"* mentioned in our opening dedication which lead the Yoga aspirant stage by

2

stage nearer to Liberation or *"Moksha"*.

In the early stages one needs to learn to control the body and thereby achieve stillness of mind by Pranayama (or breath control). This process is known as Hatha Yoga which first concerns itself with controlling the physical body *"in which we live and move and have our being."*

Swami Sivananda puts it thus, *"Raja Yoga begins where, properly practised, Hatha Yoga ends"*. Even Vivekananda, no lover of Hatha Yoga, admitted that it must play its part, *"If the body is sick, the mind also becomes sick. If the body remains healthy, the mind becomes healthy and strong."*

What is Hatha Yoga?

Before outlining what Hatha Yoga is, it must be clearly stated what it is not. Hatha Yoga is not merely the practice of physical exercises and breathing, despite the mystique bestowed by the Sanskrit terms *"Asanas" and "Pranayama"*. No fewer than seven different categories of exercises are mentioned in the classical texts on Hatha Yoga; Asanas are only one, and the science of Pranayama goes much wider than mere breath control.

The word *"ayama"* means control, but *"Prana"* in true Yoga terminology signifies much more than what we mean by breath. Prana is the universal principle of energy or force underlying all organic and inorganic matter. This primeval, cosmic force or energy is also called *"Kundalini"* - another vast subject.

Prana, in its static or dynamic form, is all-pervading. The body absorbs Prana through food, water, air and sunshine and also through subtle psychic vibrations. Conversely, the body expends Prana during every physical, mental and spiritual action.

Through regular practice of Hatha Yoga, the Yogi is

able to store an excess of Prana, just as a storage battery stores electricity. This is a useful simile, as Prana, like electricity, is said to have both positive and negative aspects which must be linked and activated before power is released.

The word *"Hatha"* is a combination of two highly significant Sanskrit syllables, or *"Bija Mantras"*, to use their proper names. *"Ha"* represents the positive or solar flow of Prana, through the right nostril, *"tha"*, the negative or lunar flow, through the left.

Hatha Yoga is a scientific and practical method of regaining and maintaining health of body and mind. It is a complete system for healthy living. It lays down a strict regime for time and place of practice, for hygiene, diet and nutrition. It prescribes specific postures (*Asanas*) to bring strength and steadiness and breathing exercises for tranquility and mind control.

The classic source books, *"Swa Samhita"*, *"Gheranda Samhita"* and *"Hatha Yoga Pradipika"*, written by Yoga Masters many centuries ago, give detailed descriptions of some of the techniques practised in the ancient world. Gheranda calls these *"the alphabet"* by which one can, with practice, *"master all the sciences"*.

In this book we have space only to glance at the letters of this *"alphabet"*. Each one is in itself a vast topic and we shall be returning to them in subsequent chapters in the book.

Nevertheless, even in this brief introduction to classic Hatha Yoga, we must make more than a passing reference to Yoga hygiene, the purification processes which are an essential preparation for a serious study of Yoga.

Kriya Yoga - Shat Karmas

In Patanjali's *"Yoga Sutras"*, the preliminary purification of the mind is known as Kriya Yoga. In *"Gheranda Samhita"*, we find descriptions of cleansing exercises - the Shat Karmas - literally, *"Six Actions"*. Kriya and Karma are synonymous, both coming from the Sanskrit root *"Kri"*, which means *"to act"*.

The *Shat Karmas* are processes to clean the body. To start practising Yoga without such cleansing is as dangerous as it would be to stitch up a dirty wound. We must eliminate toxins and impurities from body and mind, before we can practise any higher Yoga techniques. *"Cleanliness is next to Godliness"* said the old expression so familiar in Victorian nurseries, and the children were meted out *"jalap"*, scrubbed, dressed in their starchy Sunday best and marched off to Church. The six Yoga cleansing techniques were developed by the ancients to bring the aspirant constant purity of body and soul.

Today, sadly, many students - and even teachers - of Hatha Yoga have no wish to learn about the purificatory system. They are satisfied if they can master a few advanced *"Asanas"* and can sit still for half an hour or so. It must also be said that many ill-informed commentators on the ancient texts have vehemently condemned the practices as "revolting". Indeed, some of the more extreme practices are, to say the least, unsuitable for modern man, but, adapted to meet our present living conditions and practised under the guidance of a well-qualified Yoga teacher, they retain their intrinsic value as an essential step towards the spiritual goal.

I shall be returning to this topic later, but for the moment let me say that no serious student of Yoga should ignore these techniques. They were evolved over centuries of expe-

5

rience of the human body by the Masters. They destroy *"afflictions and distractions"* of the body and thence the mind. They are the very backbone of Yoga.

Let us now ask ourselves why anyone should wish to practise Yoga? What can one hope to gain? What do the writings of the Yoga Masters promise to those who practise Hatha Yoga?

Benefits of Hatha Yoga Practice

Repeatedly, we are promised that this or that practice will *"destroy diseases"*. The *"Gorakshapaddati"* tells us that, once free from all diseases, the Yogi evolves *"a lithesome body, delicate as the tender inside of the Lotus stalk, and thus enjoys youthful health and longevity"*. The Hatha Yoga Pradipika, and many of its later commentators, are no less enthusiastic, promising among other *"perfections"*, a slim body, joyous face, sonorous voice, sparkling eyes, virility and radiance. And there is more to come! Through the purification of the *"nadis"*, the nervous system, we may achieve a calm and steady mind, freedom from all signs of ageing, from failing faculties and greying hair, mastery even over death itself!

The final claim brings us once more face to face with the deeper spiritual aim of Yoga, for the *"death"* which we shall master is the death which leads us back into the endless circle of birth, death and rebirth. Exercises, however scientifically planned and assiduously practised, cannot of themselves give us liberation from past mistakes and evil actions. Raja Yoga calls not only for purity of body and mind, but also for complete purity of thought and action. Asanas, we must remember, is the third step of Patanjali's Yoga Sutras. We cannot afford to skip the first two.

Right Conduct: the "Yamas" and "Niyamas"

Perhaps it is more meaningful at this stage to use the alternative terminology, and talk of the *"limbs"* of Yoga, not the *"steps"*. For the first two limbs, the *"Yamas"* and *"Niyamas"*, make up what have been called the *"Ten Commandments of Yoga"*. They must be an integral part of every aspirant's life. They are the laws which govern dealings with one's fellow men, forming a complete code of moral and ethical behaviour which one must constantly strive to follow every waking hour.

It was the Yamas and Niyamas, as well as the higher spiritual exercises of meditation, of which Swatmarama was thinking when he said: *"Those who are ignorant of Raja Yoga and practise only Hatha Yoga will, in my opinion, waste their energy fruitlessly."* *(Hatha Yoga Pradipika, IV.78)*

SUMMARY

And so we come full circle. Asanas are part of Raja Yoga, they are also part of Hatha Yoga. Hatha Yoga in turn leads to Raja Yoga which is linked to every other Yoga. There are no demarcation lines. All paths lead to a common goal.

It is the objective of the Yoga aspirant to control and transcend the body's functions so that he may eventually eliminate all body-consciousness. Through persistent repetition of the Asanas and the preliminary and ancillary practices of Hatha Yoga, the body becomes progressively steadier, more relaxed and controlled. Then and only then, can one begin to forget the physical body and ascend the higher stages of Yoga.

Hatha Yoga is a natural remedy. Real happiness comes only with real health - and by *"real health"* we mean that

7

natural good health which is achieved without reliance on such props as stimulants and tranquilisers, vitamins and other pills. Surely it is better to practise a few simple exercises and postures daily and to follow simple laws of human nature, than to fall prey to innumerable diseases?

Let us discipline our body and mind, regularise our breathing and eating and generally control the whole pattern of our lives. Let us work to improve the health of mind and body so as to face all life's problems with strength, serenity, and happiness.

CHAPTER ONE

THE SEATED POSTURES

*"I bow to that Lord Primeval who
taught in the beginning the science
of training in hardiness....."
(Gheranda Samhita - Invocation)*

The teaching of Hatha Yoga or what Sage Gheranda refers to
as *"training in hardiness"* is an ancient oral tradition. Self-
taught Yoga or Yoga learnt from books can never pretend to be
more than the merest introduction to the subject. A long
personal teacher-pupil relationship, with instruction, demonstration, guidance, supervision and practice is essential for
success.

This is no less true of any other form of Yoga. The Hindu
scriptures abound with dialogues between disciple and Master.
The glorious teachings of the Bhagvad Gita are in the form of
just such a dialogue: *"I am Thy disciple, I come to Thee in
supplication"*, says Arjuna. The Lord Krishna smiles as He
accepts him as a pupil and, stage by stage, unfolds the message
of the paths which lead to Liberation.

The path of Hatha Yoga has many critics. It was long
despised in the East and has been condemned and rejected by
countless commentators who chose to follow other paths. I
believe that much of this criticism concerns the incorrect
practice of Hatha Yoga, which is deplorable. Some is based on
ignorance or misconceptions of its true purpose and significance. Hatha Yoga is not the performance of a series of slow-
moving exercises with fancy names, coupled with a special
type of breath control. Exclusive dependence on Asanas and

9

Pranayama is useless. Incorrect, excessive and unsupervised practice is downright dangerous.

One further warning before we start to discuss the postures. Remember always the key-note of the Gita, the call for harmony, balance and moderation. *"For him who is moderate in eating and recreation, temperate in his actions, who is regulated in sleep and wakefulness, Yoga becomes the destroyer of pain."* (Bhagvad Gita VI-17).

Swami Chidbhavananda's commentary on this verse clearly expresses our own view of the role of Hatha Yoga. *"Physical exercise,"* he says, *"as much as spiritual sadhana (practice), is incumbent upon the Yogi, but it has to be resorted to moderately....Pain is always associated with diseased body and mind. But the Yogi takes no note of the body and he is sound in mind. Therefore Yoga becomes the destroyer of pain...."*

What does Swamiji mean by *"physical exercise"*? What is the point of yogic breathing? What do we understand by Yoga postures?

Let us look at this word *"Asana"*. What exactly does it mean? What are Yoga Asanas?

Yoga, as we all know, means union. Asana means two things. An asana is both the place in which a Yogi sits and the manner in which he sits there. So the term *"Yoga Asanas"* denotes those postures by which the individual soul is helped to join the Supreme Soul, the Cosmic Consciousness, call it what you will. The practice of Pranayama aids this union and additional steps on the path of Yoga lead us nearer to meditation and our goal.

Now, let us return to look more closely at the postures. To Patanjali, *"Sthirasukham asanam"* (any steady, comfortable posture) is Asana. Lord Krishna and Sage Shvetashvatara describe both place and pose: *"Having in a clean place established a firm posture .... let him hold the body, head and neck erect and still .... let him sit with mind subdued, having me as the Supreme Goal* ".(B.G.VI,11-14). *"Meditate in a clean and level place .... a quiet spot, sheltered from the wind, not offensive, but pleasing to the mind by presence of water and gentle sound .... Hold the body still and upright, then draw the mind and senses into the heart."* (Shvetashvatara Up., 2.8).

The Seated Postures for Meditation

It is not without significance that one third of all the classical postures described in *"Hatha Yoga Pradipika"* and *"Gheranda Samhita"* are seated postures. These are the postures which give the Yoga *"kaya sthiram"*, bodily steadiness; the head, shoulders and hips in a straight line, the all-important spinal column erect to form a rock-like contact with the earth.

Squatting on the floor is a natural thing in eastern countries. To people in the West it seems, at first, odd and uncomfortable. In this chapter we shall discuss three seated postures, all are classical Yoga Asanas. Once mastered, all seem quite natural, comfortable and easy to sustain. These are *PADMAASANA*, or Lotus posture; *SIDDHASANA* or Perfect pose; and *VAJRASANA*, the kneeling position, variously translated as *Thunderbolt, Adamant, Diamond* or *Mountain* pose.

But, first, a general word about the seated postures. Western man often finds extreme difficulty in mastering the cross-legged postures. Though his basic build may be the same as that of an Oriental, cultural habits and traditions have wrought subtle differences. As Lilian Donat pointed out in an article addressed to prospective Yoga teachers, Indian mothers carry their babies straddling the hip. This may well

11

cause some early changes in the infant's pelvic girdle. (One wonders, incidentally, if the modern mum who transports her infant slung in front of her in an *"easy rider"* will perhaps be having the same effect?).

Various postures are prescribed for meditation but, in yogic practice, *PADMASANA (Illus. 1, p. 13)*, is unique and foremost. Sandilya, Gheranda, and many other Rishis speak of it in glowing terms. The full pose, from which its name derives, resembles the serenity of a full-blown Lotus - most lovely and significant of the symbols of Yoga. Padmasana is the one seated posture recognised by all who have heard of Yoga. To the man in the street, *"doing Yoga"* means sitting in a Lotus or standing on one's head. Lotus is aesthetically pleasing, compact and peaceful. Moreover, it is very important in the practice of Hatha Yoga as it is the classical starting posture for many of the advanced Asanas which the aspirant must master. For all these reasons, we are going to discuss it first.

Padmasana should not be attempted until one has developed suppleness by practising various other postures and preparatory exercises. Nor should it be performed by those suffering from sciatica or sacral problems.

A posture which is rarely mentioned in the teaching of Yoga in the West, but which is next in importance to Padmasana, is *SIDDHASANA*, or *Perfect or Adept pose (Illus.6 p.37)*. Indeed, for meditation, some Masters consider it superior. Siddhasana was the favoured pose of the *Siddhas* (Yoga Adepts) and is said to endow the practitioner with all siddhis (psychic powers). No book purporting to describe the classical asanas should ignore Siddhasana. The basic difference between the Lotus and the Perfect pose lies in the positioning of the feet. The points at which the heels press against the body are all-important in the science of Yoga practice. Why this is so will become clear as we proceed. Unlike the Lotus pose,

12

1   PADMASANA   -   The Lotus Position

Siddhasana is used only as a meditation posture. No other classical postures are performed in Siddhasana.

Another important Asana for beginners is *VAJRASANA* *(Illus. 2, p. 15)*. It has the advantage over the cross-legged postures of being easy to perform, however stiff or plump one is. It is also the only posture which can be performed after eating, while all other Asanas demand an empty stomach. This is another point which the aspirant must remember when practising, whether at home or in class. It is also a starting pose for other Asanas and Mudras which we shall describe in later chapters. This pose is used for meditation by Buddhists and Moslems.

A Basic Morning Routine

Set your alarm ten minutes earlier than usual and leave it that way for the future. After attending to your natural needs and personal hygiene, bath or shower, cleaning of teeth and so on, start your Hatha Yoga practice.

1. Dissolve half a teaspoon of salt in a basin of lukewarm water. With this cleanse inside each nostril by sniffing it up and spitting it out again through the mouth. Finally, rinse the mouth with the remaining salty water and gently blow your nose. Make sure that no water is left in the nose which can be done by moving the head from side to side. This is the simplest form of the cleansing practices known as *"neti"* and forms part of the *Shat karmas*, the six purificatory actions which every Hatha Yoga aspirant should follow.

2. Now select a clean and quiet place and take up the basic kneeling posture, *Vajrasana*.

2 VAJRASANA - THE KNEELING POSITION

VAJRASANA - THE KNEELING POSITION
ILLUSTRATION 2

Technique

The knees should be together, heels apart so that your buttocks rest on the inside of your feet. Rest the hands, palms downwards, on the knees. If it helps you, place a small cushion under the buttocks.

The body should be erect, chin slightly lowered. The position should be entirely free from strain or tension.

Exercise

Start slow, gentle breathing, making sure that the trunk, neck and head are in a straight line. On the intake of breath, the stomach muscles should relax and protrude and, on the outward breath, they should be drawn in.

3. Next practise the variation on the Vajrasana Pose as follows:

VAJRASANA VARIATION
ILLUSTRATION 3

Take up the classical *Vajrasana* position but without lowering the chin. Move the arms to the sides, palms facing outwards. Take a deep breath and raise them sideways in a gentle arc to meet in the Indian salutation position above the crown of the head.

The spine must remain completely upright. The hands should be about an inch above the head, palms firmly pressed

16

3   VAJRASANA   VARIATION

together and fingers pointing upwards. The elbows and upper arms must be pressed back to form an absolutely horizontal line and give the maximum expansion to the rib cage.

Hold the position as long as is comfortable then, exhaling gently, lower the arms in an arc.

Repeat twice more.

In later stages of this exercise the hands remain above the head with a slight relaxation of the palms on the outer breath. This is repeated several times.

This Asana gives strength and flexibility to the shoulders and helps combat stiffness in the wrists. It is also beneficial to the respiratory system.

4. Returning to the basic position move into the Counter Pose.

THE COUNTER POSE
ILLUSTRATION **4**

After every Yoga posture one should perform a counter pose. This simply means bending or stretching the body in the opposite direction.

The counter pose for seated postures stretches the legs which have been bent, allowing the blood to flow back into vessels which have been restricted.

Technique

Slowly straighten the legs and raise the body gently on the arms, as shown. Do this carefully, in the early stages it is enough to raise the buttocks a little way. Now look up.

When fully accomplished, this Asana is a variation of the Camel pose. The body is at an angle of about 45 degrees, the feet firmly on the floor, the head thrown back.

4   THE COUNTER POSE

In carefully following this short, simple routine, you will, in microcosm, have practised all the essential elements of true Hatha Yoga.

Now follow the advice given to aspirants by Vivekananda, in his little book called *"Six lessons in Raja Yoga"* :

"Be cheerful, be brave, bathe daily,
have patience, purity and perseverance.
Then you will become a Yogi in truth."

CONCLUSION

Even when one has mastered all the seated postures it is not automatic that one will remain healthier. This body is of a very complex nature, and it needs various movements to keep in good shape, as Swami Svatmarama has mentioned in his book *"Hatha Yoga Pradipika" (Ch.II-78)*. In *Chapter Two*, we will look at some of the postures which can keep this human body healthier.

CHAPTER TWO

POSTURE AND GOOD HEALTH

"Those supreme physicians, the Asvin
Twins have stated that the natural
forces relating to man can be alle -
viated by means of control of the
Prana. Therefore, O Gargi , perform
your duties in life and practise the
eightfold Yoga, observing it as a
sacred rule."
(Yoga Yajnavalkya, VIII 39-40)

In these words did Yajnavalkya instruct his wife and pupil,
Gargi and it was with this quotation that Smt. Sitadevi
Yogendra began her book, *"Yoga Physical Education for
Women" (The Yoga Institute, 1934)* addressed to the women
of the thirties.

Sitadevi spent over fity years as a practitioner and
teacher at her husband's Yoga Institute. Herself a doctor and
mother of two sons, she epitomises Yajnavalkya's teaching.
Her book, despite some rather dated terminology and illustrations, remains one of the most sound, straightforward and
helpful modern works on Hatha Yoga and its physiological
implications.

The Yoga Institute was founded by Sri Yogendra at
Santa Cruz, Bombay in 1918, at a time when in India, interest
in the techniques of Hatha Yoga was minimal and its practice
by women unthinkable. The intervening years have seen
a revolution in the acceptance of this ancient science and

21

attitudes both in East and West have changed radically. Perhaps the most significant of these changes lies in the increasing interest in Yoga shown in modern science and medicine. If, as Hindu mythology tells us, *"those supreme physicians, the Asvin Twins"* were indeed physicians to the gods and taught their healing arts to Siva, then it is high time that modern doctors began to heed their words.

Yoga and Modern Science

The modern scientist is quite understandably sceptical of the claims made for the benefits of Yoga practice. Classical treatises are frequently written in archaic language, overlaid with philosophical and religious concepts.

The practice of Yoga is of many types, *Asanas, Pranayama, Kriyas, Bandhas, Mudras* and *Meditation.* Each has complicated physiological effects on the body and psychological effects on the mind.

The human body is itself an immensely complex mechanism in which interactions occur at many levels. Many of these functions are as yet unexplained by science. As Dr. Frank Chandra, a physiologist who lectures on various aspects of Yoga, once pointed out, it is comparatively easy to make broad claims based on limited observations, subjective impressions or anecdotal evidence.

It is, however, extremely difficult to explain these diverse effects by means of theoretical models built on principles derived from modern biological sciences. Only when a generally acceptable body of documented case law and supportive evidence is available for scientific scrutiny, will medical opinion begin to take a serious interest in Yoga therapy.

It does seem, however, that there is an increasing

22

interest in submitting the results of Yoga practice to laboratory and clinical tests. The work of well-established Yoga
institutes in India and in the U.S.A. can support the benefits
of Yoga with case histories. The pioneering work of Sri
Yogendra, of Doctors Bhole, Rao Radin and others, demands
respect and points the way for further work.

Yoga is indeed a science in the full modern sense.

Yoga the Ancient Science

The ancient science of Yoga is founded on the laws of
nature. The ancients lacked access to modern methods of
research, but they had their own bodies on which to
experiment which served as their laboratory.

Yoga possesses an imposing literature of empirical
knowledge and ageless law arising from observation of how
all living things generate and conserve power and energy.
Yet these ancient texts are mere indicators of the enormous
wealth of knowledge possessed by the Masters and the
concepts of their teaching.

Why then did this rich seam of knowledge remain
obscure and unacknowledged for thousands of years?

The Hidden Teachings of Yoga

There are two main reasons for the neglect of Yoga, both
springing directly from the traditional way in which it was
taught.

Yoga has always been an oral tradition, much of it a
closely guarded secret. Only after years of austerity and
practice, when the Guru found the disciple worthy of
receiving the esoteric lore, was he taught the techniques of
Yoga. This secrecy protected the disciple from prematurely

practising the higher techniques, dangerous without proper preparation, at the same time preserving the purity of the traditional teachings.

However, the secrecy gave rise to a wealth of misinformation, ignorant prejudice and gross misrepresentation of the original and essential import of Yoga teaching and practice. Charlatans displayed their mastery over exotic postures and strange powers for monetary gain, giving rise to suspicions of magic and dangerous pagan rites.

These factors jeopardized impartial outside investigation and had built up walls of prejudice which true followers of the paths of Yoga are now attempting to break down.

In this book I am making a modest attempt to cut through the mystique which still surrounds the classical tradition. I am approaching it on the threefold front of study of the ancient texts, modern scientific thought and personal experience.

Scientific investigation of Yoga by modern observers would be most welcome if they were genuinely interested in the medical effects of yogic practices and devoted themselves to analyzing the real benefits of this ancient science. Perhaps the most obvious of such benefits is the remedial effect on postural defects.

Yoga and Posture

Asana was defined by Patanjali as the bodily position which is steady *(sthira)* and at the same time pleasant and comfortable *(sukham)*. From various references and from ancient drawings and inscriptions, it is apparent that even before the Vedic period, which scholars place at about 5,000 years ago, Asanas were known and practised.

24

Sage Gheranda tells us that 8,400,000 Asanas were described by Siva, *"as many as there are numbers of species of living creatures in this universe"*. The earliest known postures are mostly meditative poses and it is from these that the whole system of Yogasanas has developed. Meditation demands two things, a firm base for body steadiness and an erect spine for the unimpeded flow of energy known as Kundalini.

A healthy, upright spine leads to good posture. As this is a matter of crucial importance to modern man, let us look briefly at the anatomy of the human spine.

The Spine and Correct Posture

The spine consists of twenty-four (or so) moveable interverte- bral joints laid one on top of another to form a strong pillar which supports the trunk and head. It is kept erect by the facet joints and by the natural spinal curves held by taut ligamentous support. Balance is ensured by means of messages transmitted by the sense organs to the brain, any necessary adjustments being automatically effected.

The spinal cord carries the body's most important group of nerves, so proper care of the spine is essential to health. Only if the spine is supple will it be held erect without strain. It is no accident that almost one third of Yogasanas exercise the spine. In this book, we shall repeatedly return to Asanas which feature bending, stretching, twisting and relaxing the spine. Our immediate concern, however, is with the spine in stillness and more specifically, with good posture in a seated pose.

The Effect of Bad Posture

First, let us look at some of the results of bad posture, notably what one medical expert has described as *"a veritable epidemic of cervical spondylosis, disc lesion, slipped discs and all forms of backache"*. It may well be that it was this *"epidemic"* which alerted the medical profession to the implications of good posture and its effects on health, but backache is by no means the only evil consequence of bad posture.

The body's skeletal structure is designed as a protective casing for the vulnerable soft inner organs tightly packed into each body cavity. Malfunction of the organs due to pressure, overcrowding or inadequate supply of oxygen, leads to all manner of chronic complaints and lowers resistance to disease.

Causes of Bad Posture

The causes of bad posture are various and the many ills that spring from it afflict every so-called civilised society.

Badly constructed chairs can cause actual physical deformities, particularly in the young whose bones are still malleable. Beds which are too soft, malnutrition, lack of exercise, tension and emotional strain, even ill-fitting clothing and footwear, all contribute to bad posture.

Mood too can influence posture. The outer body is a mirror of the inner man. A habitual attitude of mind which is positive, cheerful and peaceful manifests itself in carriage and expression.

All this is observable and few would contest Sitadevi's assertion that *"proper carriage is essential to the health of body and soul"*.

26

Definitions of Good Posture

Rene Cailliet in his book *"Low Back Pain" (1968)* describes good posture as being *"effortless, painless, non-fatiguing, aesthetically acceptable and long maintainable"*. What could better describe Patanjali's *"Sthira sukham asanam"*?

Posture for Meditation

The classical meditation postures were designed both for the shallower levels of meditation and for those leading into the deepest realms of Samadhi, when all conscious and unconscious control of the nervous system is left behind. In these states the Yogi, unless his seat were firmly based, would be in danger of falling.

The postures are helpful even if one is merely sitting quietly with one's own thoughts, gently breathing and relaxing, withdrawing from the turmoil of daily life.

The Classical Seated Asanas

Several seated Asanas are recommended for meditation in the classic texts. The most favoured is *PADMASANA*,or Lotus Postures *(Illus. 1, p.* 13) and *SIDDHASANA*, the Perfect or Accomplished Pose *(Illus. 6, p.37). VAJRASANA,* or Kneeling pose *(Illus. 2, p. 15)* is a useful alternative for the beginner.

Alternative Positions

Swami Satyananda suggests *Sukhasana,* the *"Easy Pose",* for beginners. This is the simple cross-legged posture. It is, he

27

claims, an ideal pose for those who have difficulty in sitting in any of the classical meditative poses, but my experience has shown that it is not always helpful for Western aspirants. For someone who finds any posture which involves sitting on the floor strange and uncomfortable, a simple cross legged posture does not keep the spine erect.

Other writers make allowances for people in the West by recommending sitting upright in a chair. Here again, I have reservations. Certainly, it is better to sit in an upright chair, with the back properly supported than to slump. It is also better than to suffer acute discomfort in a mistaken notion that the agony is good for one. Yoga has nothing to do with self-torture, the aim is to forget the body, not to be painfully reminded of it.

However, when seated in a chair, artificially supported, the spine is neither strengthened nor relaxed. It is not being submitted to any new training or discipline which can effect correction or postural defects. Once bad postural habits are formed they are hard to break. The benefits of attaining the traditional seated postures are well worth the patient work needed to master them.

Physiological Effects of Posture

The classical cross-legged position gives the body a pyramidal form, the most efficient and stable model for bodily mechanics.

With hips locked, pelvis correctly positioned and the lower part of the back naturally curved, the spine is automatically held erect. The classic arm positions and hand mudras bring relaxation to the shoulders, the rib cage being then free to expand fully. The back of the neck is thus stretched and the slight forward tilt of the head is eminently restful. The posture is, moreover, an exercise in itself, the spine being strengthened as muscles and ligaments are alternately tensed and relaxed.

Cross-legged postures also have remedial and beneficial effects on the joints.

Physiological Effects on Joints

In a Paper written for the Universal Yoga and Peace Conference in 1974 (since reprinted by the Cambridge Yoga Society), Dr. Chandra highlighted several cases which illustrated the benefits of such postures. He referred to the very low incidence of degeneration of the hip-joints in Eastern people, attributed by Dr. Radin to *"the normal and frequent use of the easy Lotus Posture"*. Dr. Chandra concluded that a daily programme of Yoga, particularly exercises which rotate the hips, would, by maintaining movements in all planes and preventing capsular contraction, reduce the stiffening of the joints as one grows older. They could also improve the mobility of joints afflicted with osteo-arthritis.

Counter Indications

A word of warning! While perseverance is undoubtedly needed to achieve improvement, Yoga is harmony, it is balance and is never forced or strained.

Some medical journals, as Dr. Chandra pointed out, have illustrated the dangers of practising these postures with insufficient care. Several cases were reported of damage to the perineal nerve which is wrapped round the head of the fibula at the knee. This led to paralysis of the lower muscles of the leg and the consequent inability to lift the ankle, a condition known as *"foot drop"*.

29

Some years ago, an American doctor reported a case of a young male Yoga student who developed this condition after sitting in Vajrasana for extraordinary periods of six hours at a stretch. Also, an incidence of foot-drop was discovered among seasonal workers employed in picking strawberries and the complaint received a new name!

Other Effects of the Seated Postures

> *"He who can withdraw his senses*
> *as the tortoise draws his limbs*
> *within his shell, such a one has*
> *achieved illumination".*
> *(Bhagvad Gita II.58)*

The Masters taught that the close-wrapped position of limbs and body conserves the flow of Prana or cosmic energy. It is important for one's spiritual welfare to adopt a particular pose and reserve a special place in which one prepares oneself for meditation.

Professor M.M. Gore, Research Officer at Kaivalyadham, Lonavla, Pune, India, commenting on meditative poses writes in his book *"Anatomy and Physiology of Yogic Postures"*: *" The locking of the legs at the knee joints minimises blood circulation and prevents accumulation of blood in them...thus the nerves in this region get richer blood supply and are refreshed and toned up"*. It may be remembered that the sacral region possesses a parasympathetic network.

Measurements of electrical impulses generated in the brain have proved that the Yogi uses less oxygen when meditating. Some experiments suggest that the Asanas themselves contribute to this effect, but this is essentially a matter of conjecture.

So much for the theory, now for practice. How can we achieve the classical seated Asanas?

Preliminary Exercises

Professor Gore tells us that static postures, when the muscle tone is reduced due to the passive stretching of joints and muscles, have a soothing or tranquillising effect on the nerves. The emotions are calmed and the person becomes relaxed.

Electromyographic *(EMG)* studies at the Lonavla Ashram revealed that the heart rate did not increase more than 6% even though the maintenance of postures increased by 10% to 50%. Hence the energy cost of Asanas such as *ARDHA MATSYENDRASANA (Illus. 21, p. 95)* is reduced to a great extent.

It is not necessary that you achieve *SIDDHASANA (Illus. 6, p. 37)* in a short space of time, but persistent practice or a well-balanced routine of Yogasanas will gradually persuade the joints, muscles and ligaments to respond and stretch.

Postures, where the sole of one foot is pressed against the other thigh, are splendid hip-stretching exercises. *Illustrations 5 (p. 34) and 7 (p. 39)* respectively show *JANU SIRSHASANA,* a version of the *"Head-to-Knee Pose"* and *VRIKSHASANA,* the *"Tree Pose"* in its simple version.

Various preliminary exercises serve to remove stiffness in the feet, ankles, knees and hips. These are known as the *PAVANMUKTASANAS,* which literally means *"wind releasing postures".* They are very simple and are aimed at regulating the humours, that is phlegm *(kapha),* wind *(vata)*

31

and acid or bile *(pitta)*. This series of exercises, given below, should start your daily routine.

First, cleanse the body and try to relax both physically and mentally. Now begin your practice.

1   The Toes

Sit with legs stretched out in front of you, supporting the body comfortably with hands on either side of the trunk and leaning slightly back. Look at your toes. Wiggle them, separate them, then bend them backwards and forwards twenty times.

2   The Ankles

Flex the ankles backwards and forwards, then rotate them outwards and inwards. Later you can try cracking the ankle by rotating each in turn with the hands.

3   The Knees

Bend the right knee and clasp the hands under the thigh. Straighten the leg at a height which you find comfortable, keeping the hands firmly clasped and pointing the toes. Hold for a count of five, then flex the leg by bending and stretching it once or twice. Repeat the whole sequence with each leg in turn. Lastly, bring the foot close to the body, the knee pointing upwards. Clasp the knee and remain in this position for a count of ten. Then gently place the sole of the foot against the inside of the opposite thigh and let the knee fall outwards towards the floor. Rest the hand on the bent knee and very gently ease it downwards. You should not feel any strain in the knee joint because you are now exercising not the knee but the outward rotation of the hip.

4   The Hips

Finally, an exercise which Swami Satyananda calls the *"Half Butterfly"*. Fold the right leg and place the foot on top of the left thigh. Support the body with the left hand on the left knee. Very gently move the bent knee up and down towards the floor, letting the muscles relax as much as possible. Never strain, push or try to hasten the process. It will come in time with regular and patient practice.

Remember that, unless the body receives proper daily care, good health cannot be assured. Swami Sivananda of Rishikesh tells us to sing daily the song *"Shariram adyam khalu dharma sadhanam"* - Care of the body is truly the foremost essential thing for the attainment of the goal of human existence. While Gorakshasamhita asks the rhetorical question, *"How can one who does not know the very care of his own body, hope to achieve success in Yoga?"*
Now practise the following three Asanas:

33

JANU SHIRSHASANA - Seated Head to Knee Pose
ILLUSTRATION 5

This Asana has many physiological effects. The classical position is shown here with knee and elbows on the floor and chin resting comfortably on the outstretched leg. At first, attempt merely to rest the forehead on the knee. The bent knee is in a position which gently stretches the hip joint, excellent preparation for the classical cross-legged postures.

Technique

Bend the left leg so the heel is pressed against the perineum and the sole rests against the inside of the right thigh. Raise the arms straight up and letting the breath out, lower them so the fingers of both hands embrace the toes of the right foot. Now try to touch the right knee with the forehead. Hold for a count of ten, breathing normally, do not strain.

Now move the hands so they rest on each side of the leg. Breathe in. Raise the arms right up with the head in between.

End by lowering the arms on to the bent knee with fingers locked. Breathe normally several times. Repeat the movements on the other side.

5 JANU SHIRSHASANA - Seated Head to Knee Pose

SIDDHASANA - The Adept or Accomplished Pose
ILLUSTRATION 6

In this Asana, for physical reasons, the technique differs slightly for men and women. The heels are placed so as to exert pressure on the two important lower Chakras in order to redirect energy to the brain.

Technique

Sit with legs stretched forward. Men should press the sole of the right leg against the left thigh so that the heel presses the perineum. Women should begin with the left leg so the heel presses the cervix.

Position the opposite foot so that the heel presses the pelvic bone. Insert the toes of this foot between calf and thigh. If necessary, adjust the toes of the lower foot so that the heels rest one above the other. Legs are now completely locked, knees firmly on the ground. Place the hands in *Chin Mudra* (as illustrated) or in *Jnana Mudra* (with palms downwards).

Make sure that the trunk is straight from the waist up and that you are not slumping forward, or leaning sideways, or sitting on either foot.

6   SIDDHASANA - The Adept or Accomplished Pose

VRIKSHASANA - The Tree Pose
ILLUSTRATION 7

This is the simplest version of the classical posture. It stretches hip-joints and ligaments.

Technique

Come into standing position, arms on your side. Now raise your right leg by holding it near ankles and press the sole with the thigh and the heel as far as possible towards the perineum. With the foot placed high on the opposite thigh and knee pressed firmly backwards, balance on one leg. Stretch the arms above the head, hands in prayer position.

CONCLUSION

There is still a great deal of attention required to keep the body supple and flexible. The spinal cord (or *"Merudanda"* as it is called in Yoga terminology) is the most important part of our body. Seventy two thousand nerves which carry the energy in the human body are attached to the spine. The Yogis of yore were aware of the fact that unless the spine is kept healthy the nervous system will not function properly.

In the next chapter we will discuss how one can keep the spine supple and flexible with some Yogasanas and breathing exercises.

7   VRIKSHASANA - The Tree Pose

Maharishi Patanjali   (*Line drawing by Joanna Novy*)

CHAPTER THREE

MOTIONLESS IN MOTION
THE FLEXIBLE SPINE

"Whether young, ageing or very old;
whether sick or very frail, one who
puts aside his laziness & practices
Yoga will achieve success."
(Hatha Yoga Pradipika 1.66)

Vigorous physical exercise is for the young and fit. This is not so with Asanas, the physical postures which form an important part of Hatha Yoga. Many older people have discovered a return of youthful, vigorous health through the gentle but persistent practice of Yoga exercises. Even the far from old have felt the years slip away from their shoulders. To quote one student, after less than a year's practice, *"I was like an old lady of fifty, now I feel like a lass of twenty-four."*

In previous chapters we discussed the earliest of the postures, the seated meditative Asanas from which evolved the whole structure of the classical tradition. All such postures demand a relaxed but upright spine.

There is indeed much truth in the often quoted saying that the body is as young as the spine is supple. No cosmetic skill or tailor's art can disguise those ageing give-aways, a bent and shrunken spine, or *"dowager's hump"*. However, as we shall see, exercises in the Yoga tradition can gently coax a stiff and aching spinal column back to youthful flexibility and health.

Before we focus on the spine, we must first consider certain fundamentals. What are the essential differences between Yogasanas and other forms of exercise? What is the part played by correct Yoga breathing in the practice of postures? But first, let us see why Yoga postures are so beneficial to men and women of all ages.

The Essence of Yoga Postures: Motionlessness in Motion

Yogasanas, as we have seen, were developed centuries ago to ensure lasting steadiness and health. Every tissue is exercised smoothly, systematically and with the minimum expenditure of effort to bring about full harmony of body, mind and spirit in preparation for Realization of the Self which lies within.

The scientific system evolved by the Masters employs a unique technique which has been described as *"motionlessness in motion"*. Spine and limbs are moved into a prescribed position which is then held. During the static period of each Asana, body and breathing are stilled. This profoundly affects the whole psycho-physiological system in ways not yet adequately explained in modern science.

Motion generates energy and power. The unique discovery of the ancient Masters was that short pauses, periods of motionlessness, generate an even greater surge of energy and power. While all other forms of physical activity are, to a greater or lesser degree, exhausting, a well-balanced and conscientiously practised programme of Yogasana leaves the practitioner both relaxed and full of energy. Herein lies the therapeutic power of Yoga and the universality of its appeal.

In Yogasanas, as has been said, a cessation of breath

accompanies a cessation of muscular activity. Indeed, it is the interaction of breathing and posture which works upon the glands, organs and nervous system.

Yogasanas and Breath Control

A curious mystique has arisen around this thing called Yoga breathing. A process which should be natural, easy and an aid to both concentration and relaxation has become a controversial subject among Yoga teachers.

Some maintain that breath control should not be practised until the postural positions have been mastered, others frown on retention of breath, but I believe that it is of crucial importance that, from the outset, each posture should be learnt and practised with correct breathing. This is the only way in which the full purpose of the Asana will be achieved. The initial learning process may be a little harder, but there will be greater benefits at all stages and - most important of all - there will be no bad habits to unlearn. What will be acquired is an essential part of Hatha Yoga, that is, controlled deep breathing through the nostrils. As was said earlier, the two Sanskrit syllables which comprise *"Hatha"* refer to solar and lunar breathing through the right and left nostrils respectively.

In describing the techniques of Yogasanas in this book, I have indicated the appropriate breath control for each one. If you find it difficult to remember whilst practising at home when to breathe in and out, the "rib cage test", described later, may be of help.

Now let us turn to the main subject of this chapter, the part that Yogasanas play in spinal health.

Yogasanas and the Spine

In Sanskrit, the spine or vertebral column is called "*Meru Danda*". It shelters the main nerves of the body. Every classical Yogasana, to a greater or lesser extent, affects the central nervous system and the spinal column. All classical texts call for an erect spine for meditation and to maintain an upright spine it must be healthy and flexible.

Stiffness in back muscles leads to restricted movement, which in turn restricts and slows down the local circulation of blood. Joints, muscles and ligaments are no longer properly nourished nor properly cleansed of their waste products. Further stiffness, aches, signs of ageing and afflictions of the body's *"shock-absorbers"*, the intervertebral discs, follow.

The Intervertebral Discs

These discs are pads of tissue placed between the separate vertebrae to act as washers. They prevent friction and pressure on the spinal cord and absorb the effects of the jarring which comes from both natural and unnatural body movement.

With age, these pads of softer tissue tend to wear. If, in addition, general muscle-tone deteriorates, the blood supply of the discs is lessened and the process of erosion is accelerated. This gives rise to pressure on the spinal nerves and results in various backaches.

Acute pain from specific damage to the spine or displacement of discs calls for immediate medical attention. At this stage, Yoga has no direct part to play, but chronic backache is undoubtedly reduced by the gentle stretching

44

of the back muscles in Yogasanas. Many older people have reported an improvement in the shoulders and spine through the careful practice of the forward and backward bending of the classical postures.

The illustrations shown later in this chapter show what can be achieved when the spine is supple.

For the moment, let us look at certain exercises which even beginners can practise and which help to promote a healthy spine.

Three Simple Exercises for the Spine

These are some of the introductory exercises which follow the classical tradition. Practised regularly and with correct breathing, they will help to achieve spinal flexibility and the performance of more advanced postures.

In the next chapter I shall return to the subject of Yoga breathing and discuss the special techniques for nostril hygiene and general cleansing of the breathing apparatus. Clear, unobstructed breathing is vital to health and is central to all Yoga practice. Classical Hatha Yoga comprises many breathing exercises and postures which all aspirants should master.

SARAL BHUJANGASANA - The Sphinx
ILLUSTRATION 8

This is a simple form of *Bhujangasana*, the *"Cobra pose"*. A similar and even easier pose for the beginner is the *"Crocodile"*, in which the chin rests on the cupped hands. These gentle, backward bending exercises in the prone position are very beneficial in counteracting round shoulders and pain in the upper part of the back and neck. Chronic backache sufferers are recommended to try lying in either one of these for two or three minutes each day.

Technique

Lie face downwards on the floor, arms relaxed beside the body. Feel the straightness of your spine. Bring the hands forward beneath the shoulders, elbows close to your sides. Your first movement is a backward bend, so you breathe in. While inhaling, very gently begin to raise the head. You should feel the vertebrae move one after the other, beginning with the top one. Gradually, the weight is taken by the palms and forearms. Look up high, but do not hunch your shoulders. The lower spine, buttocks, legs and feet should be relaxed. Hold, as in the illustration, for a few seconds then, gently exhaling, lower the forehead to the floor.

Repeat twice, rising a little higher each time. Then return the arms to your side, relax and concentrate on your spine.

8 SARAL BHUJANGASANA - The Sphinx

ARDHA SALABHASANA - Half Locust Posture
ILLUSTRATION 9

Now we turn to the lower spine. The *"Half Locust"* is a strong movement which affects the lower spine and also the main abdominal organs. It is essential to take in a deep breath before raising the leg and to retain the breath while the pose is held. The full posture, the *"Locust"*, in which both legs are raised, should not be attempted by sufferers from peptic ulcers or hernia, but the simple one-legged pose, without taking the leg too high, should be suitable for most beginners. It is recommended for sufferers from lower back pain, especially one caused by pressure on the sciatic nerves.

Technique

As shown in *Illustration 9*, both legs are completely straight throughout the Asana. The clenched fists (with thumbs inside) beneath the thighs take the body's weight.

Inhale while in the prone position, hold your breath, lift the left leg remembering to keep it straight. A few inches are enough at first. Retain the breath and the pose. Exhale as you lower the leg and relax, head on one side, breathing lightly and gently. Repeat with the right leg.

9   ARDHA SALABHASANA - Half Locust Position

SARPASANA - The Snake
ILLUSTRATION 10

This is a more advanced posture. It is achieved without the support of the arms if the spine is strong and flexible.

Technique

In the prone position, with one hand clasping the other wrist, bend backwards while inhaling as in the Sphinx.

BREATHING DURING POSTURES

Every Yogasana and exercise in the true tradition of Hatha Yoga must, as has already been stressed, be practised with the proper yogic breathing if it is to have its full effect.

Some postures demand retention of the breath, others are most effective when the air is expelled. This is all very well in class when following instructions, but how do you remember when you are alone?

Here is a simple concept which may help you with your breath control while practising at home.

The "Rib-Cage" Test:

Try to associate your breathing with the position of the rib-cage. When it is *LIFTED*, as by an upward stretch or backward bend, its capacity increases and automatically air rushes in. When it is *LOWERED,* as in forward bends, its capacity decreases and air is expelled.

Do a little experiment as you read this. Incidentally, I hope you are sitting with an upright spine - you should be.

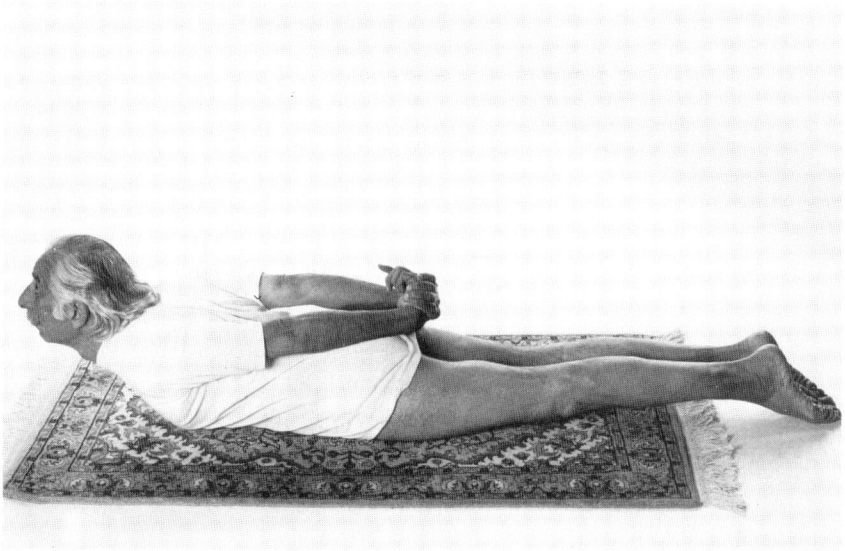

10 SARPASANA - The Snake

Place your hands below your rib-cage so that you can feel the position of the lowest ribs. Very gently bend back from the waist, do you feel that upward tilting movement? Didn't you breathe in? Now try a gentle forward bend and feel the opposite effect.

There are various Asanas and their counter poses which illustrate this movement.

You could try, for example, the graceful backward bend of *ARDHA CHAKRASANA* or *"Half Wheel Pose "(Illus. 11,p. 53)* and observe how the rib cage is lifted and lungs expanded when you breathe in.

Now try the counter pose to this, *PADA HASTASANA* or *"Head-to-Knee pose" (Illus. 23, p 99)*. The forward bend shows the opposite effect of a lowered rib-cage and expulsion of air.

11   ARDHA CHAKRASANA - Half Wheel Pose

PARIVRITTA TRIKONASANA, (Illus. 12, p 55), one of the "Triangle poses", includes both sideways bending and twisting of the spine. The movement involves strong stretching of the muscles of the trunk and rib-cage. The body prepares itself for such stretching by a deep intake of breath. On the sideways bend breath is exhaled.

We can now see how the movements of the spine and rib-cage themselves control the breathing. Yoga merely follows the body's natural breathing pattern and controls the length or breath retention.

Beginners often wonder how long to hold the breath and the posture. Here again, your own body will supply the answer if you listen to it. Treat it with respect and neither pamper nor strain it. Acquiring proper breath control, like all practice of Hatha Yoga, calls for both patience and effort. With persistence, the body will learn good habits, lung capacity will increase and concentration will improve. In addition, in listening and understanding your body you are taking a step nearer to the only true teacher, the Guru who dwells within.

CONCLUSION

We have now reached a stage where we can perform good postures, and maintain reasonable health. However, it is observed that many Yoga students and teachers alike, though with slim and flexible bodies, still suffer from various ailments such as headaches, stomach aches etc. The reason for this is not the Yoga exercises, but carelessness in their diet. The Yogis were very particular about their food and how it was prepared. We will look at this as described in a number of Yoga treatises, in the next chapter.

12   PARIVRITTA TRIKONASANA -
Revolving Triangle Pose I

Patanjali Yoga Ashram   (*Line drawing by Joanna Novy*)

CHAPTER FOUR

YOGA AND DIET

*"Bhrigu,Varuna's famous son came to his father
and said, Lord teach me the knowledge of the
Eternal.Varuna replied, 'Food, vital force, eye,
ear, mind, speech. Seek to know whence all these
take birth, that by which they live, that towards
which they move and into which they merge.
That is the Eternal." Bhrigu realised food as
the Eternal, or it is verily from food that all these
beings take birth, on food they subsist. They move
towards it and merge into food."
(Taittiriya Up. Bhriguvalli I.2)*

"Lord teach me the knowledge of the Eternal", a universal
cry which springs from man's deep yearning for some per-
manence, some point and purpose behind this transient
existence. Varuna's answer is the answer of all the Upan-
ishads, directing us to search out that immortal *"something"*
which lies within, for the Hindu scriptures are built on the
premise that mind and spirit are inextricably intertwined.
      "Everything is made of food" is a recurring theme
in Vedanta. It is not merely metaphorical, but has a practical
application also. The man who can truly see himself, not only
as an eater of food, but also as made of food and as food for
others, has moved far towards realizing the inner message of
Yoga, seeing the Self in everything and everything in the Self.
      This state of *"Yoga yuktatma"* (becoming integrated in
Yoga) brings inner bliss and spiritual ecstasy which must be
achieved while we are still living in this body which is made
of food. Through Hatha Yoga we learn to strengthen and

purify the body for the higher path of meditation and it thus follows that we must concern ourselves with diet and nutrition.

The classic works on Hatha Yoga consider every aspect of eating. A pure, light, nutritious diet is prescribed for every aspirant. They also teach that the food we eat affects both our physical and mental health.

Let us first consider the physical aspect of nutrition, man's basic food requirements for maintaining bodily health.

Diet and Health

Every living creature needs a supply of food to build tissues, repair damage, repel disease and provide the energy necessary for subsistence.

Modern chemical analysts tell us that the human body consists of a few basic chemicals worth not more than about thirty pence, but these substances must be absorbed in proper quantities, from our food. The body is designed to deal with a wide range of foodstuffs and to break them down into their constituent parts in order that they can be utilised to maintain life.

Constituents of Food - The Western View

It is currently fashionable in the Western world to take an interest in the main constituents of food. Everyone, it seems, is calorie-conscious. All have heard of proteins, carbohydrates, fats and sugars. Vitamins are glamorous, mineral salts are less so, yet many iron pills and calcium tablets are consumed each day. While in fact a properly balanced diet contains sufficient amounts of all these constituents for one's daily needs.

The scientific interest of the West in the study of food and its effects on health is of relatively modern origin. Only in the present century has any real scientific research been done on the curative and preventive effects of proper diet.

In the Eastern world the correlation between diet and health was fully understood by the Yoga Masters and known also to the medical science of Ayurveda which developed in ancient times alongside Yoga.

Constituents of Food - The Eastern View

One of the oldest schools of Indian philosophy, the Samkhya, believes in two ultimate realities, *"Purusha "* and *"Prakriti"*, each being independent of the other. Purusha is the ultimate, the *Spirit,* while Prakriti, signifying *matter,* is the unconscious principle. Prakriti is composed of three gunas or qualities, *Sattva, Rajas* and *Tamas.* They are the source of the five gross elements of *Pancha Mahabhuta,* that is *Ether, Air, Fire, Water and Earth.*

Ayurvedic medicine and Yoga are both concerned with the whole man, body, mind and spirit. Terminology and emphasis may differ, but their roots and aims are one.

Food and Nutrition according to Ayurveda

Sushruta, a medical practitioner of Ayurveda in ancient times says, *"The trinity of gods namely, Water, Fire and Air create, uphold and sustain the material universe. Similarly, the self-same trinity of the three gods named as Vata (wind), Pitta (bile) and Kapha (phlegm) maintain and nourish the miniature universe of our body".* *(Sushruta Samhita Ch.21, V. 8)*

Food and body being matter, both consist of the five basic *"bhutas"* or elements. Different foods have differing proportions and combinations of these elements, some of them more beneficial to the body than others.

As we discussed earlier, Ayurveda maintains that it is essential to the health of the body and mind that the *"doshas"* or humours (*bile, phlegm and wind*) are kept constantly in equilibrium and that different foods profoundly influence this balance, affecting general health and bringing changes in attitude, mood and, over a longer period, personality.

Sage Gheranda, in his treatise on Hatha Yoga, recommends that an aspirant eats *"foods which nourish the humours of the body"*, but the science of Yoga takes this further, stating that the food we eat affects our spiritual progress also, for food is intimately connected with the mind and intellect.

Food and Nutrition According to Hatha Yoga

Yoga teaches that *"food, once eaten, becomes three-fold"*. Grossest particles are rejected, finer ones become the flesh and the finest particles become the mind. Sage Uddalaka puts it thus, *"When curds are churned, my son, fine particles rise upwards as butter; similarly, when food is consumed fine particles rise up to form the mind." (Chandogya Up.6.6).* The Chandogya Upanishad also says, *"Through pure food the inner nature is purified" (7.26.2).*

Food and the Gunas

In order to comprehend the yogic attitude to food, we must once more speak of the three *gunas*. Throughout Yoga practice one must constantly remember that one's aim is to reach the tranquillity of the sattvic guna for, as Lord Krishna tells us, *"When sattva asserts itself, wisdom arises". (Bhagvad Gita Ch.14 V.17)*

According to Hatha Yoga certain foods are capable of

changing the predominance of a particular guna in the individual. The Masters, therefore recommend that one chooses one's diet carefully from a range of sattvic foods.
How are we to recognise such food?

Sattvic, Rajasic and Tamasic Food

In the *Bhagvad Gita (Ch.17 V 8-10),* Lord Krishna says that food that is dear to all is of three kinds:-
Sattvic food is that which prolongs life, brings purity, strength, health and happiness. Food which is savoury, substantial and agreeable.
Rajasic food is bitter, sour, saline, overhot, pungent, dry and burning. It brings pain, grief and disease.
Tamasic food is stale, tasteless, ill-smelling, cooked and left overnight, putrid and impure. Swami Chidbhavananda, commenting on the food which is cooked and then left overnight, says that one should use one's discretion with regard to this as certain food cannot be used immediately after cooking whereas others ought to be consumed shortly after preparation. Any food can become tamasic - none is so by nature - although one modern commentator may well be justified in calling alcohol and narcotics tamasic food.
"Yoga Pradipika" and various other Yoga classics give examples of rajasic foods which the aspirant should avoid. Common to all lists are acid, fermented or salty dishes, meat and fish. Certain berries and certain *"heavy"* vegetables are also interdicted. Garlic and onions also figure on most lists. These are over-stimulating foods which rouse passions and interfere with spiritual progress. It is fairly easy, therefore, to compile a list of classical prohibitions for Yoga diet. It is less easy to find the list of recommendations.
Commenting on the *"Gheranda Samhita"*, Ma Yogashakti tells us that many of the listed sattvic foods are no

longer recognizable from their classic names and descriptions, even in the country of their origin. In order, therefore, to decide upon a sattvic diet one must consult more modern Masters.

In his *"Practical Lessons in Yoga"*, first published in 1938, Swami Sivananda gives a comprehensive list of sattvic foods - and very wholesome and attractive they sound:- dairy produce, grains and cereals, honey, nuts, dried ginger; a wealth of fresh fruit and vegetables and salad stuffs; dates, figs, raisins and sugar candy. All natural, simple food.

Is there then a Yoga diet which all aspirants should follow?

A Yoga Diet

Much unnecessary agitation is caused by searching for a universal Yoga diet. No such thing can possibly exist. The dietary needs of the serious aspirant, following a path of prayer and meditation within the confines of an ashram will be entirely different from those of one who leads a physically energetic life. Yoga diet needs to become a part of sadhana, a spiritual practice.

As *Yoga Tattva Upanishad* tells us, *"Those proficient in Yoga should give up food detrimental to the practice of Yoga"*. So much is obvious, but what of the beginner practising Asanas? Must he at once alter his whole eating pattern and attitude to food? No, this is not necessary. Sudden changes are rarely beneficial to the body, drastic changes in diet can do more harm than good, both to general health and to Yoga practice. Changes in diet should be introduced gradually when body and mind are properly prepared and ready for them.

As one progresses on the path of Yoga, one may find that the need for meat, stimulants or sedatives will decrease and cravings for certain foods, alcohol or cigarettes diminish. Nothing could be better, but let it happen gradually, without strain or guilt.

Each aspirant should therefore select the diet best suited to his Yoga practice and development. Are there any rules of Yoga diet which have a universal application?

What Yoga has to teach about diet falls into three categories. Let us consider each in turn.

First, Yoga is concerned with the quality of the food we eat and secondly, with quantity. Finally, and that which is perhaps most important, Yoga is concerned with our mental attitude to food.

The Quality of Food

The quality of food is all important to the Yoga aspirant. Lord Krishna in the Bhagvad Gita tells us, *"foods that prolong life and increase purity, vigour, health, cheerfulness and happiness, are those that are soothing, substantial and agreeable."* *(Ch.17, V.8)*

So much for quality, what of quantity? What is really meant by "moderation"?

The Quantity of Food

Classical Hatha Yoga treatises are explicit and at times elaborate in instructing the aspirant on this controversial subject *"Abstemiousness"*, we are told, *"means that three quarters of hunger is satisfied"*. *(Hatha Yoga Pradipika Ch.I V.58)*. Other sources recommend filling half the stomach with food, leaving a quarter of its capacity for water, and a quarter for *prana-vayu,* the energising air which digests it.

These appear to be comfortingly precise rules for quantities until one begins to consider the problem more

63

carefully. Each of us knows the feeling of a full stomach, even more do we recognise when we have had too much, but three-quarters? Half full? How are these quantities to be assessed? Once again, it seems, we are thrown back on our own resources. Each must assess for himself the quantity he eats. Certain techniques have been devised to help us control the intake of food and I shall return to these in *Volume 2*, but the most efficient method is the use of Prana.

Control of Prana is central to all Yoga practice, for Prana is that all-pervasive vital energy by which we live and breathe. Certain techniques of *Pranayama* (Yogic breathing) specifically help to overcome hunger and thirst. For the present, let us attend to the interaction between Prana and food.

In the science of Ayurveda, Pranavayu is the vital air which helps us to digest our food. In our opening quotation from the *Taitiriya Upanishad*, Bhrigu realizes food as the Eternal. Later, he comes to realize Prana also as the Eternal for it also is food.

Hatha Yoga teaches us to eat frugally and leave space in the stomach for Prana. The Masters teach that the slow, deliberate chewing of food both releases more Prana from the saliva and utilises more fully and efficiently the Prana present in the food itself. Thus, it is argued, if we eat more slowly, we shall improve digestion, require less food and feel less hungry.

Hunger, however, is subjective. It does not necessarily indicate a physical need for food. The senses, eyes, ears and nose may trigger off a *"need"*. An emotional need for comfort, relief from tension or boredom may well signal *"I am hungry"* and the overworked computer of the brain is tricked. This is where the full power of Yoga is needed for constant vigilance and control of mind.

64

Mind over Matter - Mental attitude to Food

Yoga *"inhibits the modifications of the mind"*, Patanjali tells us in his second Yoga Sutra *"Yogaschitta vritti nirodhah"*. Regular and persistent practice of the full techniques of Hatha Yoga will gradually help us to control the mind and the senses. As Vyasa, the great commentator on Patanjali has put it, *"Yoga can be known only through Yoga"*.

We must constantly apply the central teachings of Yoga to the whole subject of diet and nutrition. Varuna taught that food and Prana, eye, ear and mind are all to be realized as the Eternal. Let us then learn to use the inner eye, the inner ear and consciousness to control our attitude to food. Eat whatever foods you wish, but remain the master. Do not crave any special diet, however *"good"* or *"sattvic"* you may think it. Becoming a slave to a new type of diet will not help your spiritual progress. Live a simple life and enjoy simple food if you can, but do not take up a *"holier than thou"* attitude. Never worship food, but never despise it. Practise detachment.

The Sannyasin with his begging bowl is not offered a selection of carefully prepared, fresh, sattvic food, but he is master of his mind and senses. So concentrated is he that he can draw Prana from his meditation and live a healthy life on any food.

As Swami Sivananda says: *"He who lives to eat is a sinner, but he who eats to live is verily a saint"*.

One rule relating to eating is mandatory on every practitioner of Hatha Yoga. The stomach must be completely empty before performing Asanas. At least four hours should elapse after a meal, two to three after a light snack. This is the reason why early morning, when the whole digestive process is completed, bowels emptied and personal hygiene done, is the pre-eminent time for practising Asanas.

This chapter illustrates the positions of *Shashtanga Surya Namaskar (Illus. 13, p. 67)* - *"Obeisance to the Sun with Eight Points of the Body"*, or the more familiar translation, *"Salutation to the Sun"*, mentioned in the Rig and Yajur Vedas. This rhythmically flowing exercise, with its controlled breathing and recitation of Mantras, has been practised daily in India for thousands of years. It embodies a technique for opening up the body to the cosmic energy which emanates from the sun.

Surya Namaskara is not, strictly speaking, part of the classical tradition of Hatha Yogasanas, but is an important adjunct to them, with its special bearing on the digestion and utilisation of food, breathing, balance and most of all, on cultivating the correct mental attitude of concentration and awareness.

In the full practice of Surya Namaskara, *"Surya"*, the Sun, is worshipped in all its splendour as Lord of the Heavens, symbol of spiritual Light, the Eternal, the Self in all. Each of the twelve positions has its own Mantra, praising a different aspect of the life-giving power of solar energy. This does not make it a religious rite or practice, although positions and their accompanying Mantras have a deep spiritual content. Sri Apa Pant, in his excellent little book on Surya Namaskara promises the regular practitioner that *"Slowly but surely...... you will feel the full force of beauty and harmony, unity and oneness with all that is"*. This is the promise of Yoga.

With or without Mantras, this wonderful exercise should always be practised with full awareness of every part of the body. Become the seer of every movement, avoid distractions, take the mind within.

In the illustrations of the positions of Surya Namaskara you will find the description of each pose, the movement into the next position in the sequence and the recommended

13   SHASHTANGA   SURYA   NAMASKARA

breathing. Once mastered, the whole sequence should flow smoothly and naturally. The Mantra which accompanies each position is also given. These Mantras are usually repeated when moving into the position. If taught and practised properly they can have a profound effect.

The sequence should be repeated several times. Once completed, relax in *Savasana (Illus. 14, p.75)*, for several minutes with slow regular breathing.

It takes a little time to memorise the sequence and to train the body to perform the movements properly. The following pairs of positions are the same:-

1 and 12,   2 and 11

3 and 10,   4 and 9

5 and 8

The beginner may find it helpful to learn the sequence in three separate stages:-

Stage 1

Take up Position 1, *PRANAMASANA*. Move into Position 2, *HASTRA UTTANASANA*. Move into Position 3, *PADAHAS-TASANA*. Then back into Position 2 and thence to Position 1.

Repeat several times and practise for several days before trying the second stage.

Stage 2

Take Position 3 and perform the sequence of Positions 3 - 4 - 5 - 4 - 3. Again, practise this stage for several days.

Stage 3

Take up Position 5 and perform the sequence as follows:

5 - 6 - 7 - 8.

In many ways this is the hardest stage but, once mastered, you will soon be able to tackle the whole sequence of Surya Namaskara. Your body will recognise the stretching and contracting of the muscles, the breathing rhythm and the benefits of the full sequence.

1   PRANAMASAN - Prayer Pose

MANTRA : OM MITRAYA NAMAH
Salutations to the Friend of All.

Stand erect, feet together, facing the rising Sun. Bring the palms into the prayer position. Gently close the eyes and relax the body, feeling the point of balance. Breathe deeply and gently. Feel at peace.

Movement to Next Position

On the outward breath open the eyes and take the hands forward and downward to touch the front of the thighs. Immediately, breathe in and swing the arms upwards and backwards, shoulder-width apart. Arch the trunk and neck as far back as possible into the second position.

2 HASTA UTTANASANA - Raised Arm Pose

MANTRA : OM RAVAYE NAMAH
Salutations to the Shining One.

This backward bending posture stretches the viscera, works on the stomach muscles to remove excess fat, extends the rib cage and tones the spinal nerves.

Movement to the Next Position

On the outward breath swing the arms and trunk forward and downward, head between the arms, to place the hands on the ground in the third position.

3 PADAHASTASANA - Head-to-Foot Pose

MANTRA : OM SURYAYA NAMAH
Salutation to Him who induces activity.

With legs as straight as possible, head close to the knees and the abdomen fully contracted to expel any remaining air, this is a splendid posture to aid digestion and elimination. It helps to keep the spine supple and tones the nervous system.

Movement to Next Position

Breathing in, take the left foot back, raise the trunk and head into the fourth position.

4   ASVA SANCHALANASANA - Equestrian Pose

MANTRA : OM BHANAVE NAMAH
Salutations to Him who illumines

Arch the spine backwards and then look up. The arms should be straight, hands firmly on the ground. Abdominal organs are massaged, the nervous system balanced and the leg muscles strengthened.

5   ADHOMUKHA SVANASANA- Dog Pose

MANTRA : OM KHAGAYA NAMAH
Salutations to the One who moves quickly in thesky

Breath should be completely exhaled, eyes focused on the navel. Contract the stomach muscles and keep the feet flat on the ground.

Movement to the Next Position

Teachers differ on both the method of moving into the sixth position and the position itself. Some teach that the knees should touch the ground first and others that the buttocks should be raised in the sixth position. I prefer to let the body flow in a smooth rhythmic movement into the sixth position with first chin and chest, then the whole trunk, touching the ground. Thence move equally smoothly, into the seventh position. The movement begins on an inhalation and breath is retained until the body is in the seventh position.

6 SHASHTANGA NAMASKAR
Salutations with the eight limbs

MANTRA : OM PUSHANE NAMAH
Salutations to the Giver of Strength

The body remains only briefly in this position with the breath retained. In this version, the weight is still on the hands and toes and the body is straight without raising the buttocks.

Movement to the Next Position

Taking the weight on the hands, swing the trunk upwards and straighten the arms into the seventh position.

7 BHUJANGASANA - Cobra Pose

MANTRA : OM HIRANYAGARBHAYA NAMAH
Salutations to the Golden Cosmic Self

The arms are straight, the whole trunk arched deeply backwards, eyes looking upwards. The toes are still firmly on the ground. The lungs are completely filled with air. This posture strengthens the spine, arms and shoulders and is beneficial to the lungs.

Movement to the Next Position

On the outward breath, swing the buttocks up into the eighth position, transfering the weight to the legs.

8 ADHOMUKHA SVANASANA - Dog Pose

OM MARICHAYE NAMAH
Salutations to the Lord of the Dawn

Follow Position 5

Movement to the Next Position

On a strong inhalation, bring the left foot forward between the hands, bending the right knee and taking the trunk and head back into the ninth position.

9 ASVA SANCHALANASANA- Equestrian Pose

MANTRA : OM ADITYAYA NAMAH
*Salutations to the Son of Aditi, the
Limitless One*

Follow Position 4

Movement to the Next Position

On the outward breath, bring the right foot forward between the hands into the tenth position.

10 PADAHASTASANA - Hand-to-Foot Position

MANTRA : OM SAVITRE NAMAH
Salutations to the Benevolent Mother

Follow Position 3

Movement to the Next Position

On an inhalation swing the arms and trunk up into the eleventh position.

11 HASTA UTTANASANA - Raised Arm Pose

MANTRA : OM ARKAYA NAMAH
Salutations to Him who is fit to be praised

Follow Position 2

Movement to the Next Position

On exhalation bring the hands down into the prayer position, which is the twelfth position.

12 PRANAMASANA- Prayer Pose

MANTRA : OM BHASKARAYA NAMAH
Salutations to the One who leads to enlightment

Follow Position 1

Relax, gently close the eyes and take a few deep breaths. Now repeat the whole sequence, but taking the right foot back when moving into Position 4 and bringing the right foot forward when moving into Position 9.

You have now completed half a round (from the left) of Shashtanga Surya Namaskar. You should perform not less than three whole rounds, more if you have the time and the stamina.

Finally, rest completely relaxed in *Savasana ("Dead*

74

14 SAVASANA - *Dead Man Pose*

Man Pose", Illustration 14, p. 75) with slow, regular breathing, for several minutes.

CONCLUSION

We have, to an extent, now understood the benefits of classical Yoga postures and the kind of food one should eat to maintain bodily strength. However, it will not be of much use if we do not know the process of eliminating the waste matter from the body. If the body is not cleansed of impurities, they can obstruct the flow of vital forces within and slow down our progress towards higher aims. The next chapter shows a number of Yoga practices which help to eliminate waste and make the body a proper instrument to achieve our goal in Yoga.

CHAPTER FIVE

YOGA AND ELIMINATION

The alimentary canal in the human body can be compared to a stream which, when impeded, will exude foul air and contaminate the atmosphere around it. In the same way, many ailments arise in the body when proper elimination is impaired.

Rishi Gheranda, author of *"Gheranda Samhita"*, when explaining the science of *Ghatastha Yoga* (Yoga based in the body) to his disciple, King Chandakapali, says that seven types of exercises need to be practised for the attainment of the seven accomplishments, the first of which is a pure body. Ma Yogashakti, commenting on this stanza, says in her book, *"Yoga Syzygy"*, that *"without purification of the body one can never be fit to pursue the path of higher Yoga"*.

The Shat Karmas

The *Shat Karmas*, as has been said before, form part of the basic preparation for Yoga. *"Saucha"* *(cleanliness)* is first among Patanjali's five observances for the Yoga aspirant. Saucha means cleanliness of thought, word and deed. The Shat Karmas have been described as *"the physical methods of cleansing the inside of the body which is the temple of the spirit. (Hatha Yoga Pradipika Ch.2 v.21)*.

Three of the six actions concern digestion. *Dhauti*, which cleanses the upper part of the digestive tract from tongue to stomach, *Vasti*, a type of enema, and *Nauli*, a method of massaging and stimulating the intestines.

77

The traditional methods of practising Dhauti and Vasti are seldom practised in the West today. The modern approach to internal cleansing of the intestines will be discussed later in this chapter. Nauli, however, belongs not only to the Shat Karmas, but also to regular Hatha Yoga. The *"Pradipika"* recognizes Nauli to be the most useful of all Hatha Yoga practices. It is indeed uniquely effective in certain cases of constipation.

In *"Gheranda Samhita"* we are told *"to move the stomach to both sides with force"*. In her commentary on this description of Nauli (or *"Lauliki Yoga"*, as Gheranda calls this technique), Ma Yogashakti advises personal demonstration and careful supervision. *"You may get an idea of it from a photograph"*, she says, *"but its practice is very difficult"*.

However, three safe and simple techniques have been evolved for the modern practitioner. Each helps gently to stimulate the peristatic muscular action of the colon.

Simple Forms of Abdominal Massage

The colon, or large intestine rises from the right side of the lower abdomen, crosses beneath the diaphragm and descends to the left. The first technique consists of gently massaging the whole of this tube. The second concentrates on the top of the ascending and descending colon where the contents enter and leave the upper transverse portion. This, incidentally, are just those points where the elbows are pressed into the abdomen in the *Peacock pose (Illustration 18, p. 89)*. The third is specifically intended to stimulate the flow of blood to the abdomen.

1 Massage of the Whole Colon

Lie on the back and gently knead the abdomen with a rotary movement, following the clockwise direction of the colon. Begin the kneading low down on the right hand side of the abdomen, working up the ascending colon to the lower ribs and across the horizontal portion to the left. From there, massage down the left, descending part of the colon. Repeat several times. Some authorities suggest taking a glass of hot water before this is practised. Others advise that lying on the floor may help. Find the positions and method that suit you best.

2 Massage of the Transverse Colon

Massage of the two side portions of the transverse colon can be comfortably performed even when sitting in a chair. It is safe for the elderly and frail and has been found effective in cases of chronic looseness of the bowels as well as in chronic constipation.

Sitting upright in a chair, put the hands on the hip bones, thumbs behind and fingers pointing towards the navel. Gently but firmly squeeze and relax the abdomen. Repeat as many times as you find comfortable.

3 Sahaj Agnisara Dhauti

This technique, which has been found most effective, is regularly practised in Indian Ashrams. Its purpose is to stimulate a healthy flow of blood to the abdominal area.

Kneel in *VAJRASANA* *(Illustration 2, p. 15)* or sit cross-legged. Place the hands on the hips, thumbs above the hip bone but below the bottom rib, fingers on the navel. Without moving the thumbs, press the navel towards the spine and quickly release it. Repeat this at least thirty or forty times.

No chapter relating to Yoga elimination would be complete without mention of *Shankha Prakshalana*. This is the complete internal washing of the digestive tract.

Shankha Prakshalana

Shankha Prakshalana is a form of Dhauti. *"Shankha"* means a conch shell (the supposed shape of the intestines), while *"Prakshalana"* means *"to completely cleanse"*.

A full programme of complete intestinal washing takes several hours and must be undertaken under guidance of a competent Yoga teacher. A special diet must be followed both before and after the process. It would not normally be performed more frequently than two or three times a year. However, a form of it, namely *Laghu Shankha Prakshalana, (Illustration 15, p. 83)* can be practised daily if necessary until the body is accustomed to eliminating regularly and efficiently.

Laghu Shankha Prakshalana

Early in the morning, before eating or drinking anything, prepare a hot salty solution (two teaspoons of salt to two litres of water). Drink two large cupfuls of this salty water, as hot as you can stand and as quickly as you can. Then, immediately perform the following six exercises, which swirl the salty water round the stomach and intestines.

Each exercise should be repeated eight times and then the whole process should begin again, with two more cups of hot salty water. It should be performed three times in all. Thus, six cups of water all together have been used to flush out the system.

Remember to repeat each one eight times.

1 Stand with feet together, hands stretched upwards, fingers clasped with palms facing the ceiling. Lift and lower heels quickly.

2 With feet about 18 ins. apart, arms still above the head, bend sideways as far as you can to the left and then to the right.

3 Bend forwards, legs apart, arms in front pointing to the floor. Turn the body as far as possible, first to the left and then to the right.

4 Stand with feet apart. Take the right hand behind the head to rest on the left shoulder-blade and the left hand on the other shoulder-blade. Turn the whole body from left to right and then from right to left. At the same time, first turn the left foot to the right and then the right foot to the left, in time with the body.

5 Go down into the position for press-ups with feet together. Taking the body weight on your straight arms, with legs straight and toes on the floor, twist the body so as to look over your left shoulder at your right foot. Then repeat the process in the other direction.

81

6 Finally, come into a squatting position on your toes. Swivel the body round from left to right, keeping your back upright, then from right to left. (You may fall over at first, but don't worry, everybody does).

Sometimes you may get an immediate desire to evacuate the bowels or it may take a while, but the salty water will be doing its work. If nothing happens do not worry, at least your kidneys will be flushed out and healthier than before. Try again next day. Reforming habits needs patience and perseverance.

Constipation occurs when the bowel movements are infrequent. That much is obvious, but what also happens is that elimination is incomplete. So, many who believe themselves free from this complaint, are nevertheless suffering from it. Curing constipation is a lengthy business. The whole of the digestive tract, from tongue to rectum, must function properly. This entails a complete cleansing of the whole system and retraining of the body.

The Ill-effects of Constipation

It is claimed that 95% of disease in modern man springs from constipation and faulty diet.

Constipation arises from the inefficient action of the bowels in passing waste products which remain after all the nutriments, (in Yoga terms, the *Prana*) have been absorbed from the food and passed into the bloodstream.

The large intestine, or the colon, is a tube with elastic walls. The passage of its contents towards the rectum is effected by the bands of muscle which surround those walls. When waste is not regularly and efficiently expelled, the muscles become weak and loose and the colon stretched. Good bowel movements, moreover, should consist of some

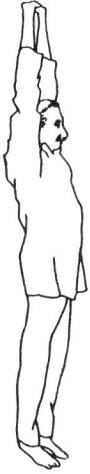

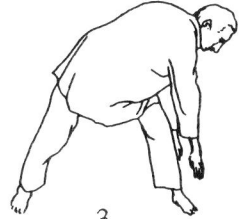

2

3

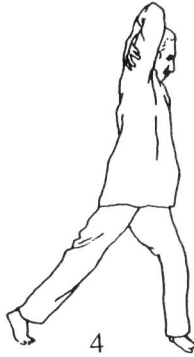

1

4

6

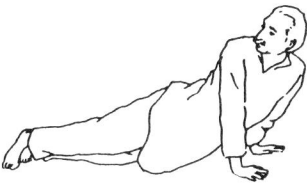

5

15 THE SIX EXERCISES OF LAGHU SANKHA
PRAKSHALANA

75% moisture. According to the science of Yoga complete evacuation of the bowels should take place before sunrise. This is rarely practicable in modern life, but irregularity and delay in emptying the bowels on rising render the stools dry, hard and difficult to pass. Moreover, particles of the faeces may remain in the bowels, setting up further complications and diseases which range from the simple headache to disabling rheumatic complaints. Purgatives may give temporary relief, but for the most part they work by irritating the nerves and mucus lining of the bowels. This, in turn, sets up further constipation and aggravates the condition. It is, therefore, of the utmost importance that the muscles are kept in tone, which is greatly helped by the practice of Asanas.

Remedial Yogasanas

A regular and balanced programme of Yogasanas, practised for some fifteen to twenty minutes a day, will steadily rebuild the muscular strength of bowel walls. Several postures which have been found to be effective are illustrated here, but there are many, many more.

Almost every standing, stretching exercise will help to combat constipation. Squats and twisting exercises are extremely helpful. Exercises which compress the viscera in forward bending, followed by extension in a backward bend are also useful. It is unwise, however, to hold the position of a strong forward bend, such as the seated head-to-knee pose, Paschimottanasana. This can inhibit bowel action and tends to cause further constipation.

Sufferers from chronic constipation must also avoid the full headstand, Shirshasana (Illus.16, p. 85) until the condition has been corrected by other means. Instead, they should substitute the simple inverted pose, Viparita Karni

16 SHIRSHASANA - The Head Stand

condition has been corrected by other means. Instead, they should substitute the simple inverted pose, *Viparita Karni Mudra (Illus. 17, p. 87)* which helps the process of elimination.

Even the simplest of all Asanas, *Vajrasana (Illus. 2, p. 15)*, the Yoga kneeling posture, is recommended. Kneel in this posture for a short time after every meal. It might cause comment in a busy restaurant, but what is there to stop one trying it at home?

Let us then look at some Asanas that are particularly useful in combating digestive disorders.

Mayurasana: The Peacock Pose (llustration 18, p. 89) is one of the most efficient of all Asanas in promoting good digestion and encouraging bowel movement. However, of the many who suffer from digestive disorders few can hope to master this difficult posture. Indeed, to many of us the very threat of having to perform it would be sufficient to deter us from further over-indulgence.

Hatha Yoga Pradipika describes this Asana as follows:-

"Place the palm of both hands on the ground and press the elbows into the navel. Balancing thus, stretch the body out straight as a rod" (Ch.I, 32-33).

To the Hindu, *Mayur*, the peacock is a sacred bird. Lord Krishna wore its feathers in his headband. It graced the lawns of palaces and temples, while its feathers were used as ornaments and fans. To the pragmatic Ruskin, the peacock seemed one of *"the most beautiful things in the world"* and yet *"the most useless"*. To William Blake, it was *"the glory of God"*.

Yoga postures are said to have been first taught by Lord Siva, and peacock was the vehicle of one of his sons,

17 VIPARITA KARNI MUDRA - Inverted Pose

Karttikeya. Therefore, it is fitting that one of the most valued of classical postures bear its name.

Mayurasana, the Peacock Pose, is said to be imitative of the heavy body of the bird steadily balanced on its seemingly frail and stick-like legs. In the advanced version *(Illus. 19, p. 91),* the legs are lifted high in the air imitating the spread of the peacock's fan.

One commentator has suggested that the connection between this posture and its curative effect on constipation is that peacocks can kill snakes and the posture *"kills"* poisonous waste in the body. Others interpret the reference to poison in more spiritual ways. All agree, however, that *Mayurasana* is one of the most effective ways of improving digestion.

Disorders of the body originate in the mind. The degree of awareness and tranquility which the aspirant derives from Yoga practice as a whole, therefore, contributes greatly to the healthy elimination of wastes from the body.

On the physical level, almost every Yogasana, correctly performed, will affect the function of the viscera, the complex system of organs and glands within the abdominal cavity and stimulate them to greater efficiency. Moreover, the Yoga cleansing processes, breathing exercises, diet and fasting also have their part to play. All are vital to the retraining of the bowels which is the only lasting cure for constipation.

MAYURASANA I - The Peacock Pose (ILLUSTRATION 18)

Technique

Kneel with feet together and knees apart. Place the palms flat on the floor between the knees, fingers pointing towards the feet. Lean forward to rest the abdomen on the elbows,

18 MAYURASANA I - *Peacock Pose*

which should be close together and placed each side of the navel. The chest should rest on the upper arms. Stretch the legs straight behind you. Toes on the floor.

Exhale and raise one leg from the floor. Inhale and lower it. Repeat with the other leg. Now exhale, tense the leg muscles and raise both legs and trunk to the horizontal position, finding the point of balance. Hold, then slowly lower the legs as you inhale. Take a few natural breaths before repeating.

MAYURASANA II - Advanced Peacock Pose
ILLUSTRATION 19

Once the first position has been mastered and can be held for some time with natural breathing, the advanced version may be attempted.

Technique

Come into *Mayurasana Pose 1.*

Raise the legs gradually higher and higher in imitation of a peacock's fan. Be sure that the weight is still on the elbows; resist the temptation to press the chest on to the upper arms, which makes breathing laboured and difficult.

19   MAYURASANA   II   -   Advanced   Peacock   Pose

PURNA MATSYENDRASANA - Full Spinal Twist
ILLUSTRATION 20

This is one of the most aesthetically pleasing of all Asanas and also the most beneficial. Its name comes from its *"inventor"*, Rishi Matsyendra Nath, a quasi-mythical figure mentioned in the *"Pradipika"* as one of the founders of *Hatha Vidya* (*knowledge*). He is said to have meditated in this posture for many hours at a stretch.

Part of the benefit of the *Full Twist* lies in the pressure exerted by the heel on the lower bowels, but even the simplest of twisting Asanas helps to massage the internal organs of the body. It relieves abdominal disorders by compressing and twisting the alimentary canal and has beneficial effects on the genito-urinary system. The twisting of the spine is also most beneficial in certain types of chronic backache.

Technique

Sitting upright with the legs stretched in front of you, place the right foot on the pelvis as in the *Lotus Position*. Lift the left foot over to the right side of the right knee, sole firmly on the ground. Raise the right arm up and over the raised left knee, twisting the body as you do so and grasp the left foot. At the same time, on the outward breath, take the left arm and place it on the floor behind your back, twisting your trunk and head round to look over your left shoulder. Breathe deeply and naturally in this position holding it as long as possible before repeating the procedure on the other side.

A difficult pose, but one which can be mastered with practice and perseverance.

20 PURNA MATSYENDRASANA - Full Spinal Twist

93

ARDHA MATSYENDRASANA - Half Twist
ILLUSTRATION 21

Technique

Sitting with legs stretched in front of you, take the right leg over the left and place the foot flat on the floor beside the left knee. Bend the left leg to place the heel against the right buttock. Place the right hand on the floor behind you at first, to serve as a support. Now, bring the left arm over the upright knee to catch hold of the right foot or ankle. Breathe out and, using the straight left arm as a fulcrum, twist the trunk towards the right, taking the right hand behind your back as you do so. Try to touch the left thigh. Breathe gently in the posture and then return to the starting position and repeat the other side.

21 ARDHA MATSYENDRASANA - Half Twist

USHTRASANA VARIATION - *Camel Pose Variation*
ILLUSTRATION 22

A very simple twisting movement, a variation on the Camel Pose.

Technique

Sit in Vajrasana, knees a little apart. Rise into a kneeling position, arms at the sides. Breathe in and raise the arms sideways and outwards to shoulder level. On the outward breath gently twist the torso to the left, swinging the left hand downwards to take the weight on the right heel. The right arm swings high into the air. Look up at your hand. Hold for as long as comfortable, breathing gently, then back to the starting position. Repeat in the other direction.

Repeat twice more and then return to *VAJRASANA* and take 30 deep breaths with full concentration on the movements of the abdomen, paying special attention to the indrawn tummy muscles when breathing out. This relieves tension as well as providing a gentle massage for the abdominal muscles.

22   USHTRASANA   VARIATION
Camel Pose Variation

97

PADA HASTASANA - Standing Head-to-Knee Pose
ILLUSTRATION 23

Technique

Stand upright, hands by your sides. Exhale and bend gently
forward and down, allowing your hands to hang forward
towards the ground. Bend as far as you can without forcing.
Come up, breathing in.

23 PADA HASTASANA
Standing Head to Knee Position

99

CHAKRASANA - Wheel Pose
ILLUSTRATION 24

Technique

Stand upright with hands at the sides and feet 18" (46cms) apart. Take a deep breath in and start bending the legs and arching the spine backwards slowly. Make sure your neck muscles are relaxed and the back of the head is close to, or touching the shoulders. Now try to touch any part of the back of the legs or ankles. As soon as the hands are resting on any part of the leg, start normal slow breathing, maintaining the balance of the body all the time.

A word of caution. This Asana should not be done if there is any dizzy feeling, which may be due to stiffness of the neck muscles or nerves. Before you attempt the Wheel, practise the other exercises recommended in this book.

24 CHAKRASANA - The Wheel Pose

PARIVRITTA TRIKONASANA - The Revolving Triangle
ILLUSTRATION 25

Technique

Stand with feet 3'- 4' (92-123 cms) apart. Stretch your arms sideways at shoulder level. Turn the body to the left, exhale and with arms in a straight line bend to touch the left foot with the right hand. The left arm remains in a straight line above your head. Now, look up at the palm of the left hand. Hold the position.

Breathing in, come back into the upright position. Repeat on the other side, keeping arms and legs straight.

CONCLUSION

Most sincere and conscientious aspirants try to follow the rules and principles of Yoga in their lives, but the sense organs are so powerful that they are influenced by them and become slack in their routine/discipline. This generally occurs when one crosses the line of moderation and indulges in excess. The result is over-eating and neglect of physical Yoga postures which leads to over-weight or obesity. In Ayurveda it is called *Meda-rog* (disease of the fat), and can cause an obstruction to an aspirant in their progress. Our last chapter deals with the control of weight problems if and when they arise during Yoga practices.

25   PARIVRITTA TRIKONASANA
The Revolving Triangle Pose

Sri Indar Nath in *Padmasana* or the *Lotus* position.

CHAPTER SIX

YOGA AND WEIGHT CONTROL

*"Verily Yoga is not possible for
him who eats too much , nor for
him who eats too little, but for
him who regulates his food and
recreation, Yoga becomes the
destroyer of pain".
(Bhagvad Gita Ch.VI, 16-17)*

In our opening quotation, Lord Krishna gives Yoga's strategy for healthy weight control in simple, direct terms. He tells us not to eat too little, not too much, and to balance our activity with rest. This is no annual skirmish with an ever-spreading waistline, but a constant manning of the ramparts against all enemies of health.

The practical techniques of Hatha Yoga, perfected over countless ages, develop health and harmony in every dimension of man's being. Through control of the body comes the stilling of the mind. Yoga does not focus merely on the physical body, whatever shape it may be, it focuses on the Self within.

The Way of Moderation

To live without excess, to find and hold steadfastly to the middle path which lies between the pairs of opposites, the two extremes, is Yoga's recurrent theme, the way of moderation.

This is no easy option. Indeed, the *Kathopanishad* describes the middle path as *"the razor's edge"* so difficult to tread. The word *"moderation"* must not be used as an excuse when faced with some unattractive task or when justifying some indulgence. To follow the way of moderation requires persistence, self-control and the courage to face hardships, but as Rieker says in his commentary on *"Hatha Yoga Pradipika"*, *"Life is never hard if I am not too soft"*. As steel is toughened in the furnace, so the fire of hardship strengthens man.

Practice of austerity is incumbent on the Yoga aspirant. In the Yoga Sutra it is called *"Tapas"*, which means *"to heat"*. A burning determination is required to face the hardships of Yoga's battlefield of life. Determination is equally needed in the battle of the waistline, as permanent weight control demands a totally regulated and moderate way of life.

In this chapter you will find the application of the Yoga rule of moderation to the question of weight control. Yoga believes that if there is inner goodness, self-discipline and moderation in all actions, then good health, grace and harmony manifest themselves.

Control of weight demands a balance between input in the form of nourishment and output in the form of energy. Lord Krishna asks for moderation in both. Let us first consider Yoga teaching for moderate eating.

Moderation in Eating

> *"A slim body is one of the first attributes necessary to acquire perfection in Hatha Yoga".*
> *(Hatha Yoga Pradipika II,77)*

Obesity is one of the most prevalent of modern problems although its dangers were fully recognised by the prac-

106

titioners of Ayurveda, the ancient Indian science of longevity, which has its roots in the Vedas. A modern medical assessment of obesity is that each pound of excess weight may mean one month less of life. On the other hand, fear of obesity can lead to drastic measures for reducing weight which are equally damaging to health.

Obesity has many causes, such as glandular malfunctioning, heredity or cultural influences, but by far the most common cause is simply overeating. However, to view this problem as merely a lack of self-control is negative and ill-founded. Overeating may arise from basic insecurity, anxiety or grief, boredom, frustration or anger far more often than from gluttony. Eating habits have deep emotional roots.

Following a life of moderation through Yoga gradually helps to develop a comfortable, healthy attitude to this problem. The individual finds a way of breaking through the endless cycle of compulsive eating alternating with starvation which he has adopted to compensate for the psychological problems he does not recognise.

Yoga treats the weight problem for what it is, an illness which requires a total remedy. It prescribes new habits to replace the old. The first stage in the treatment is to cleanse the system of the impurities accumulated through bad eating habits, thus making way for a fresh start.

Changing One's Habits

Saucha, that is cleanliness of body and mind, is a vital part of Yoga. Shankha Prakshalana, the inner cleansing method described in *Chapter Five,* is an excellent preliminary to a change in eating habits. It flushes out the system, leaving an encouraging feeling of lightness to give an initial impetus to the task.

A more fundamental approach involves a period of fasting and it is to this aspect of inner cleansing that we now turn our attention.

Yoga and Fasting

Fasting is not a remedy for obesity but nature's remedy for disease. Swami Sivananda Ji says in his book *"Health and Happiness"* that fasting is a curative measure of great importance and is an effective speedy remedy for many ailments. The ritual practice of fasting is prescribed by every great religion to purify the mind for spiritual advancement.

On the physical level, nothing eliminates waste products more efficiently than a fast, but it must never be allowed to become starvation. Fasting is a voluntary abstention from food for a controlled period and its effects are invariably beneficial. Starvation, on the other hand, is imposed and uncontrolled. Overeating strains the body while undernourishment can result in death.

Every living cell is expending energy, even during periods of quiescence. It is equipped to store up nourishment on which to draw when food is not available, hence man's basic biological urge to eat more than his immediate needs dictate. Obesity arises when he habitually stock-piles a greater store of fat than he can utilise. On the other hand, there are certain vital elements which the body cannot store. If these requirements are witheld, deficiency diseases appear. Many young people today put much effort into restricting their intake of food below acceptable limits, thereby ruining their looks and threatening their health.

Systematic self-starvation is no modern phenomenon, nor does it solely arise through vanity. In every generation, earnest seekers after Truth, following rigorous asceticisms, have carried the practice of *"Tapasya"* too far in the mistaken notion that it hastens spiritual growth. *The Chandogya Upanishad (6.7)* describes the ill-effects of prolonged fasting on Svetaketu's memory (not one word of the Vedas could he remember), while the modern *"Kundalini Yogi Gopi Krishna* " describes periods of self-mortification.

"The proficient in Yoga", says the Yoga Tattva Upanishad, *"should give up....emaciation of the body due to fasting"*. Practice of ascetism for ascetism's sake is expressly condemned in the Gita, *"Those of demonic nature who mortify the body excessively"*, says Lord Krishna, *"outrage Me, the Dweller in the body". (Ch.XVII, 6)*

The attitude of Yoga to fasting is one of moderation, of keeping to that narrow middle path, while the return to food is considered to be far more important than the fast itself. It must be done very gradually and in accordance with the duration of the fast. The stomach will have shrunk and the digestive organs will be unable to cope with any but the smallest and lightest of meals at first.

Longer periods of fasting, says Swami Sivananda Ji, may be necessary to cure chronic or prolonged illness, but it should be done under guidance.

Moderation in Eating

Mitahara (moderation in eating), is according to *Hatha Yoga Pradipika (Ch.I, v. 52), "foremost among the Niyamas"*. Mitahara literally meaning *"less of eating"*, is an integral part of Tapas.

"Take pure, sweet, cooling foods to fill half the stomach", says Sage Gheranda *(Gheranda Samhita V, 21-22), "eating sweet juices thus with pleasure is called moderation in eating."*

According to the science of Yoga, nothing is difficult when you know how to do it. Certainly, the classic instruction to allow space to be left for Prana in the stomach becomes progressively easier with practice. Experience soon demonstrates the pleasant feeling which follows a light and nourishing, sattvic meal, from the dull heaviness that follows over-cramming with tamasic or rajasic foods.

Taking smaller meals with smaller helpings, fewer courses and no nibbling in between, not only establishes better eating habits and digestive health, but also adds to the sheer enjoyment of the taste of food. Chewing every morsel slowly helps both the taste and the digestion of food. The most enjoyable part of eating begins outside the body. First the eyes and nostrils *"enjoy"* the food, then the taste buds and the tongue. Once the food has passed into the throat, its flavour has already undergone a change and enjoyment ceases. It is a sad truth that many compulsive eaters bolt their food and never really savour what they eat.

Incidentally, the yogic practice of rinsing the mouth immediately after eating is not only an excellent piece of oral and dental hygiene but also prevents the tongue from craving more of the same, or different, foods.

So much then for the all important subject of moderation in eating, the first part of Lord Krishna's recipe for yogic health and weight control. How can Yoga help to increase the efficiency with which the body utilises the energy from the food or, in modern terms, the metabolic rate?

Yoga and the Metabolic Rate

Every person has a basic metabolic rate which determines the speed and efficiency with which the body effects the digestion and ingestion of food and utilises the energy it produces. This rate varies greatly, not only from person to person, but also in each individual. Age, health, glandular efficiency, climate, life-style, even mood affect the rate of metabolism.

In terms of modern science, the metabolic rate is controlled by nervous impulses which, in their turn, control the secretions of the endocrinal glands. In terms of Yoga this is done by conserving and utilising different forms of pranic energy in the body.

Almost every *Yogasana* and *Pranayama* influences the nervous system and glands. All affect the metabolic rate. *Mudras* and *Bandhas* also affect the health and harmony of the body, mind and psychic structure.

Yogasanas and Weight Control

According to the Hindu scriptures, Lord Siva taught his wife, Parvati, 8,400,000 Asanas. Over the centuries this number has shrunk to a small fraction of the original. Some thirty postures are considered beneficial to modern man.

For the healthy working of the endocrinal system and stability of weight, nothing could be better than a carefully balanced daily programme chosen from this small group. The more proficient one becomes in performing Asanas, the longer one is able to hold the all-important static stage and the smaller the number of postures required.

Sarvangasana, or *Shoulderstand (Illus. 26, p. 112)* for example, peformed with such control and balance that the body remains relaxed and upright, unsupported by the hands, produces profound effects on the thyroid gland. This gland, perhaps more than any other, directly affects body weight. A long-held Sarvangasana, followed by a backward bend such as *Matsyasana* or *Fish Pose (Illus. 27, p. 113)* will thoroughly massage and activate the thyroid gland as well as

111

26 SARVANGASANA - *Shoulder Stand*

27   MATSYASANA - Fish Pose

113

bring countless other benefits to the body.

Backward-bending Asanas from the prone position, produce strong effects on abdominal glands concerned with metabolism and digestion. *Salabhasana* or *Locust Pose* *(Illus. 28, p. 115)*, in particular, is one of the most efficient ways of stimulating the production of adrenalin and insulin, two important factors in weight-control.

Classical postures are gentle, well-tried, natural and, like nature, they work deliberately and slowly. The aspirant who is well taught, patient and has persistence to practise the postures daily, will certainly normalise his weight.

Many who come to Yoga primarily for the physical benefits, tend to find the initial stages frustrating and unrewarding, because when they come they are still out of condition, over-weight and in a hurry. Many modern Masters, therefore, have devised exercises to help the beginner to progress towards the practice of Yogasanas.

This approach to the teaching of Yoga had its inception in India, the home of Yoga, in modern Yoga institutes and schools where the therapeutic properties of Yogasanas have been studied in the light of modern medicine and ancient tradition. The exercises have been given Sanskrit names and are taught in the classical way, with full awareness of the body. They use slow, deliberate movements, correct breathing, pauses and relaxation.

Experience has shown that, in the long run, nothing can be as effective as the ancient postures and that these modern exercises should be seen simply as a practical introduction to Yogasanas.

In contrast to my normal practice of describing the techniques and benefits of classical postures, in this Chapter you will find examples of modern introductory exercises. All of them will help you to acquire flexibility and encourage

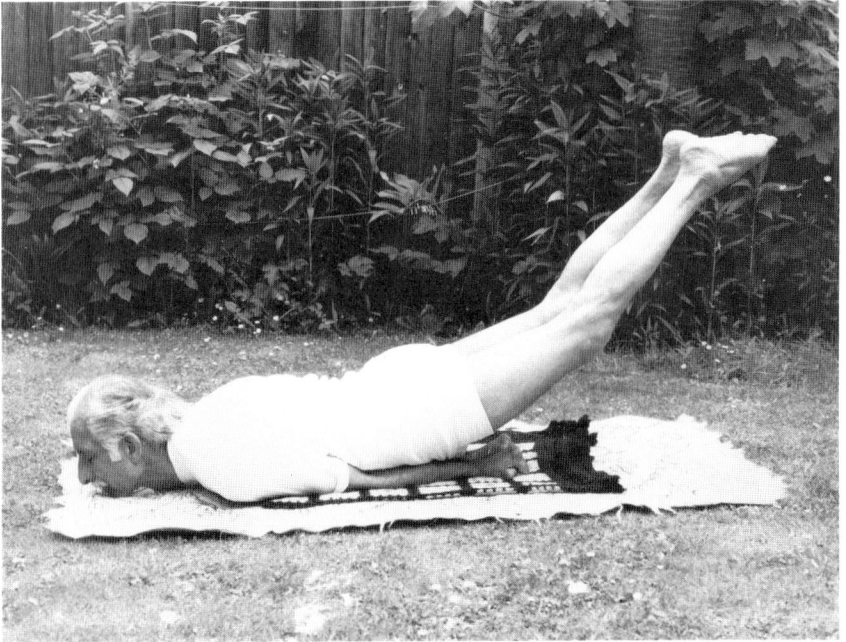

28   SALABHASANA - Locust Pose

115

weight-control. Use them as a spring-board for achieving the classical positions.

Introductory Callisthenic Exercises

These have been devised and adapted by some of the modern Yoga Masters to help beginners to ease some of the stiffness arising from the accumulation of toxins. All are performed slowly and deliberately, with correct breathing in the classical manner and lead directly towards the performance of traditional postures. Different stages of these exercises are shown with their English names.

LEG RAISING EXERCISE
ILLUSTRATION 29

An all-round toning-up exercise, preparatory to the inverted postures.

1   Lie on your back, feet together, hands by your sides.

2   Inhale, bend the knees and bring them up towards the chest. Exhale.

3   Breathing in, straighten the legs and hold them steady in the vertical position. Breathing out, slowly lower the legs to the ground.

Repeat three times.

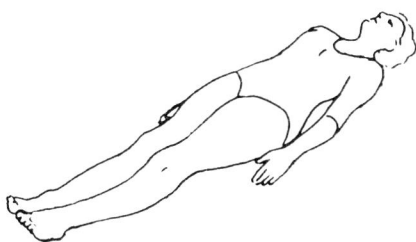

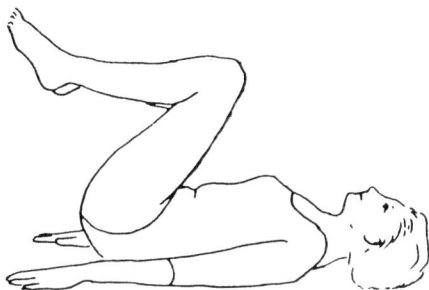

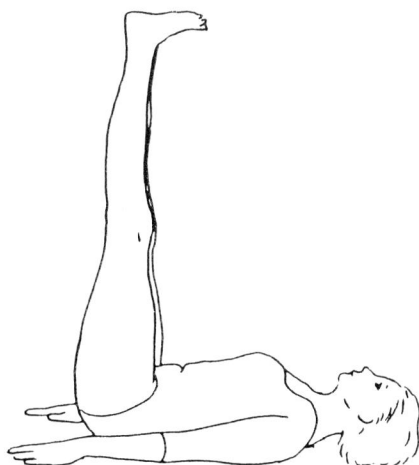

29   LEG RAISING EXERCISE

SIT UP, LIE DOWN EXERCISE
ILLUSTRATION 30

This is another useful exercise for strengthening weak muscles and massaging the abdominal organs.

Sit up and lie down again several times from a fully stretched position without the help of hands or elbows and without bending the knees.

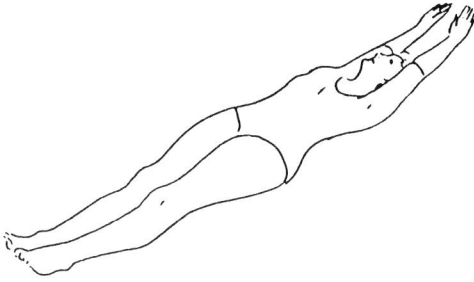

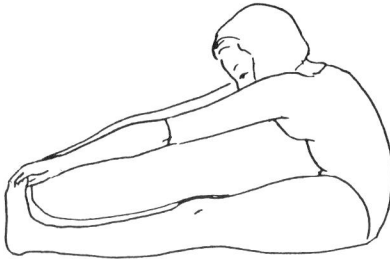

30   SIT UP, LIE DOWN EXERCISE

BUTTOCK WALK EXERCISE
ILLUSTRATION 31

1   Sit with legs straight out in front of you, hands resting on the thighs.

2   Bend forward and catch hold of the toes.

3   Lift the left leg and buttock from the floor and *"walk"* forward.

4   Repeat with the right.

Take four *"steps"* forward on each buttock, then four back again. Good for increasing flexibility in the hip area and for slimming the buttocks and waist.

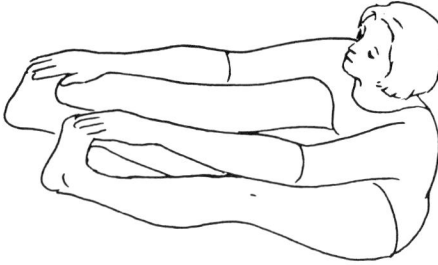

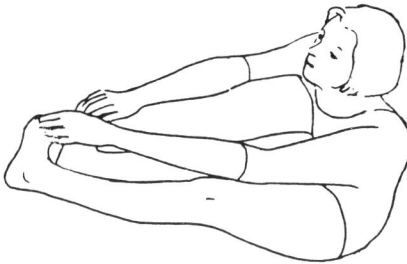

31   BUTTOCK WALK EXERCISE

HUG AND STRETCH EXERCISE
ILLUSTRATION 32

1   From the same position of sitting with legs stretched in front of you, bend the knees and bring the feet in towards the buttocks.

2 Pass the arms under the thighs and clasp the elbows with the hands.

3   On the outward breath, slowly slide the feet forward, keeping the chest as close to the knees as possible.

4 In the final position bend forward, legs straight in front of you and the elbows and forearms to the ground.

This is an excellent stretching exercise in preparation for the many important forward bending Asanas which are so beneficial in the relief of abdominal ailments.

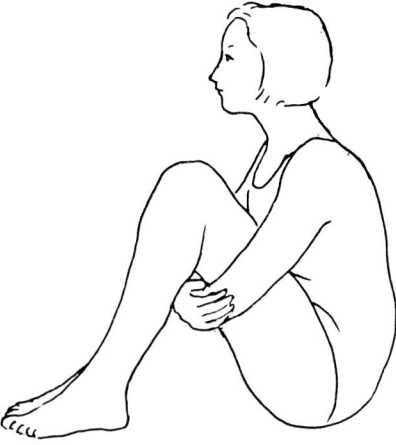

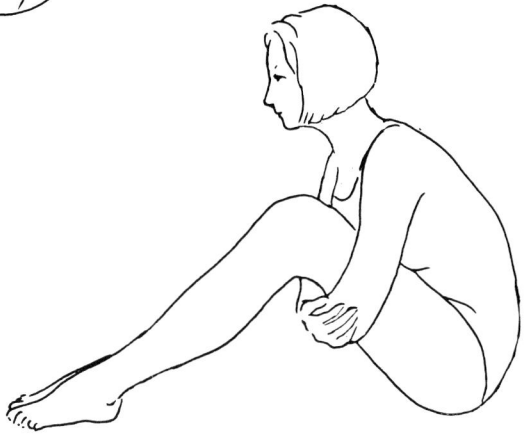

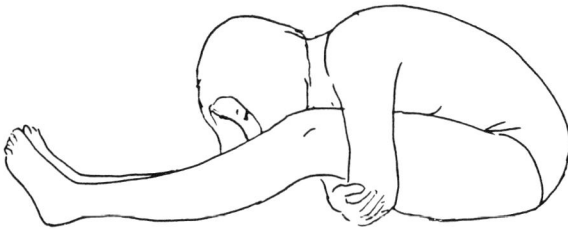

32   HUG AND STRETCH EXERCISE

THE STARFISH EXERCISE
ILLUSTRATION 33

This exercise is often included in a beginner's programme to help bring flexibility to the spine in preparation for backward bends such as the *Cobra, Locust or Bow* poses.

1 Lie on the floor spreadeagled on your stomach. On the outward breath first raise and lower each arm in turn, then each leg.

2 Now proceed to a diagonal posture: simultaneously raise first the right arm and left leg, then the left arm with the right leg.

3 Finally, try the complete *Starfish Pose:* Lie on your stomach on the floor with arms and legs outstretched without touching the floor.

Hold as long as possible with the breath retained.

33   THE STARFISH EXERCISE

Pranayama and Weight Control

The practice of Pranayama, of which more will be said in *Volume 2,* should always be learnt from a competent teacher. It is a vital part of Hatha Yoga, with potent physical and psychological effects. *"An individual who has mastered yogic breathing",* says the *Trishikhi Brahman Upanishad, "achieves full control over the senses, requires less food and sleep, becomes strong physically and mentally and achieves longevity".* Pranayama, according to *"Gheranda Samhita",* requires that one keeps to a light diet. *"If one starts to practise without regulating one's diet one is bound to suffer from several diseases and will not meet with success".* *(Gheranda Samhita V, 16).*

The practice of Pranayama helps to control the mind. As has already been mentioned, most weight problems originate in emotional imbalance. Generally speaking, every practice that helps mind control and relaxation will also help weight control.

Practice of Pranayama also affects the metabolic rate. Moreover, two of the classical Pranayamas are specifically said to reduce hunger and thirst. Both involve inhaling through the mouth, which is unusual in Yoga breathing.

SHITKARI PRANAYAMA - The 'Hissing' Breath
ILLUSTRATION 34

This is practised by placing the tip of the tongue behind the teeth and inhaling through slightly parted lips, making a slow, hissing sound. It is often called *"the hissing breath".* Exhalation is through the nostrils.

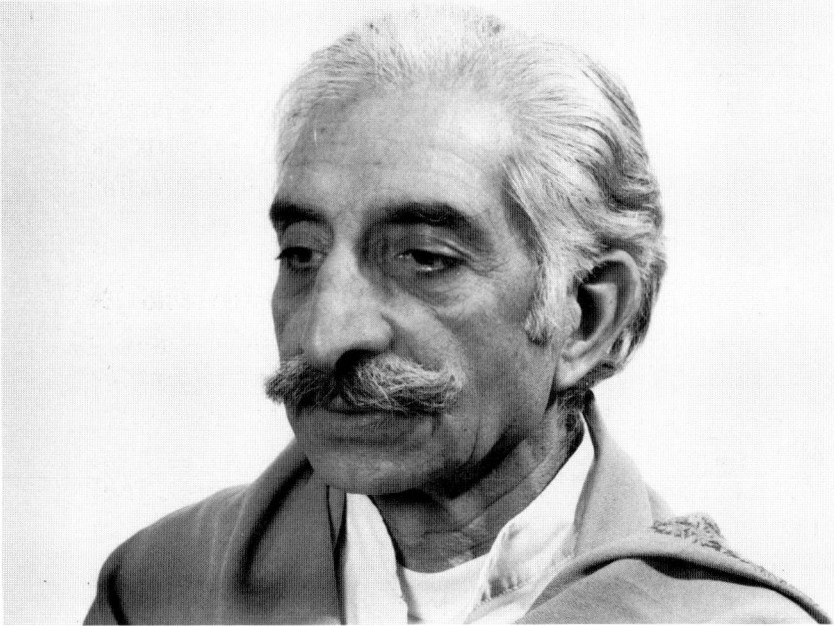

34   SHITKARI PRANAYAMA - The 'Hissing' Breath

SHITALI PRANAYAMA - The 'Cooling' Breath
ILLUSTRATION 35

This is usually called *"The Cooling Breath"*. In *Shitali Pranayama*, the inhalation is made through the protruding tongue, its sides folded upwards to form a funnel. Some liken it to the beak of a bird. Inhalation is slow and deep. The tongue is then withdrawn and placed behind the upper teeth for a short time, with the breath retained, before exhaling slowly through the nostrils.

As in all Yoga breathing, the rhythm is of utmost importance. It must be slow and regular. Exhalation must always exceed inhalation. Classically, it should be twice as long. Retention of breath is not important in the early stages.

This Pranayama figures in both *"Siva Samhita"* and *"Gheranda Samhita"*, as also in the *"Hatha Yoga Pradipika"*. It is said to aid digestion, *"cure cough and bile troubles"* and *"to appease hunger and thirst"*. *"Shitali Pranayama"*, says Gheranda *"is very good for everyone"*.

Certainly, the compulsive eater, who suddenly feels the urge to nibble at something, would benefit if, instead, he practised a few rounds of Shitali Pranayama.

Finally, let us look at the effect on weight of the practice of *Uddiyana Bandha*.

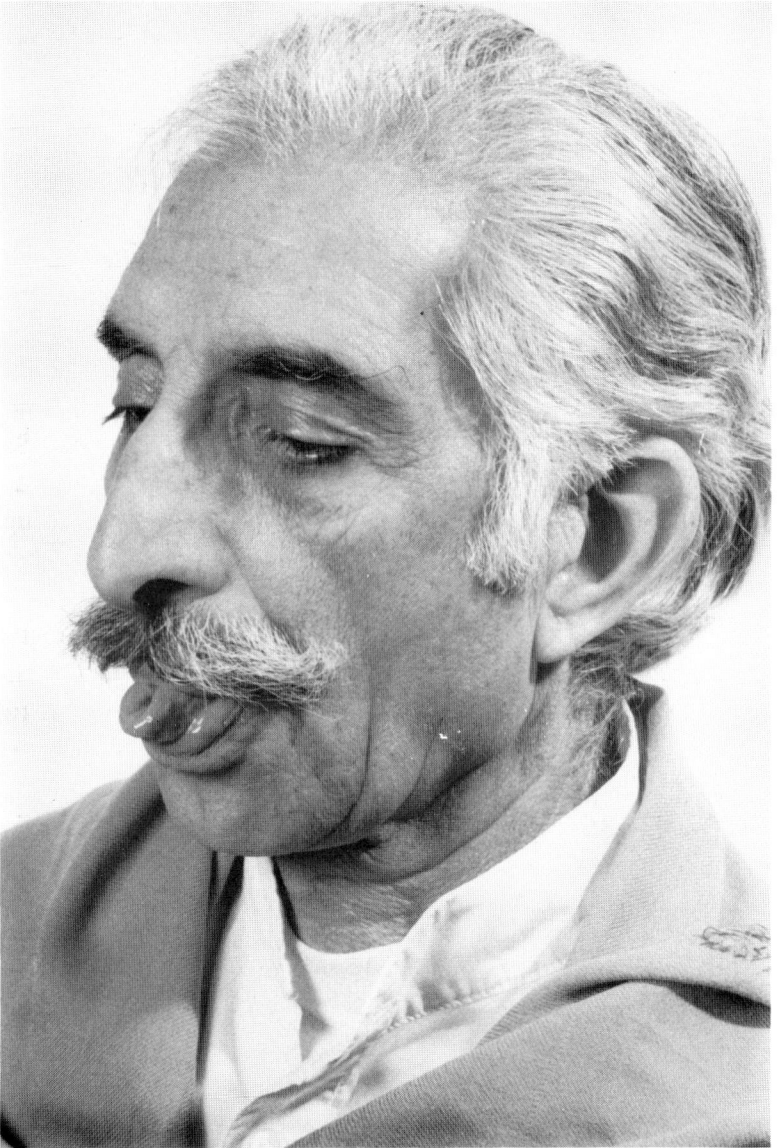

35   SHITALI PRANAYAMA- The 'Cooling' Breath

Uddiyana Bandha and Weight Control

"Uddiyana" literally means "to fly up". It is also the modern Hindi word for an air-flight.

Uddiyana Bandha, The Abdominal Retraction Lock (Illus. 36, p. 132) is considered to be the foundation of all advanced work. Some Masters even believe that it should be perfected by the practitioner as early as possible. In her commentary on the *"Gheranda Samhita"*, Ma Yogashakti tells us that all diseases caused by irregularities in diet are alleviated by this practice. Its benefits are, she says, *"beyond evaluation"*.

In *Kundalini Yoga*, the performance of this Bandha allows a great surge of psychic energy to fly up the *Sushumna Nadi,* the channel situated inside the spinal column. *"Hatha Yoga Pradipika"* mentions Uddiyana in three separate sections.

As part of the purification process by *Shat Karmas*, as an adjunct to Pranayama and finally, in meditational practice. *"Of all the Bandhas"*, says the *Pradipika (Ch.III,60), "Uddiyana is most excellent"*.

"Bandha" means to tighten or to hold. The Bandhas form a small but most important group of Yoga practices. Various groups of muscles are systematically contracted, thus massaging internal organs, accelerating hormonal secretions and stimulating and toning the nervous system.

In *Uddiyana Bandha* there is a strong contraction of the abdominal organs concerned with digestion and assimilation and of the large network of ganglia nerves which affect the central nervous system. Hormonal secretions, particularly from the adrenal glands and the pancreas, are activated. All are concerned with metabolism and thus *Uddiyana* is a helpful practice for weight control.

Uddiyana Bandha is an extremely beneficial basic classical practice of Hatha Yoga. Not only is it, of itself, a most important exercise, but is an essential preliminary to many of the higher practices.

However, here is a word of warning. Uddiyana Bandha should *NEVER* be performed after eating, nor by those with any *SERIOUS ABDOMINAL DISORDER*, nor *DURING PREGNANCY* or *HEAVY MENSTRUATION*.

Three different postures are shown here in which this exercise may be performed. The basic technique remains the same for all of them.

UDDIYANA BANDHA - The Abdominal Retraction Lock (Standing) - ILLUSTRATION 36, P. 132

This is the easiest position for beginner.

Technique

Stand with feet about 9 ins. apart. Bend slightly forward and place the hands on the front of the thighs, pressing firmly to support the body's weight. Exhaling deeply, draw the abdominal muscles firmly inwards and upwards. Lower the chin to press into the hollow of the throat *(Jalandhara Bandha or Chin Lock)*. Hold as long as comfortable, then slowly release the muscles, raise the head and inhale. Take several deep natural breaths before repeating. Do not practise more than three times at first.

36 UDDIYANA BANDHA
The Abdominal Retraction Lock: Standing

UDDIYANA BANDHA II - Abdominal Retraction Lock in Seated Posture (ILLUSTRATION 37)

Choose a firm meditation position. Make sure that your pose is steady and place the palms over the knees. Now proceed as before.

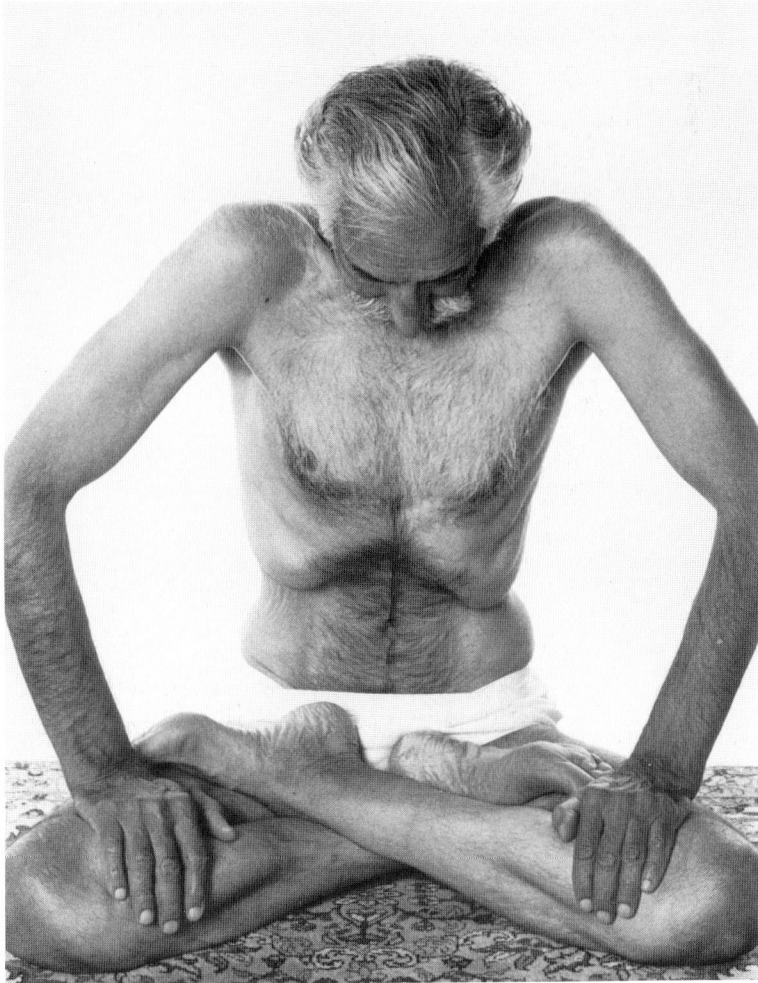

133

UDDIYANA BANDHA III   Retraction Lock in Cat Pose
(ILLUSTRATION 38)

Uddiyana Bandha in this pose is an excellent exercise for the stomach muscles, especially   for   restoring tone   after childbirth.

CONCLUSION

We began our introduction with the opening *sloka* (verse) from Swami Svatmarama's book, *"Hatha Yoga Pradipika"*, in which he emphasises that the only way to Raja Yoga is through the mastery of Hatha Yoga.

From the first commentary on *"Hatha Yoga Pradipika"* by Jyotsna in 1893 to present day commentators, it has been made clear that Hatha Yoga is not a set of physical exercises, but the control of Prana within. In *"Gheranda Samhita"*, which is an earlier treatise on Hatha Yoga, the great Master Gheranda refers to the attainment of seven qualifications for a Yoga aspirant. The first two are a pure body and a strong mind which can be acquired by purificatory exercises and Yogasanas respectively. *(Ch I, 9-11)*.

Some of the present day teachers and Gurus overlook the fundamental physical disciplines and the systematic practice of Pranayama and so feel reluctant to pass them on to their students and disciples.

It is interesting to note that, in an introduction to *"Hatha Yoga Pradipika"* (published by the *Theosophical Society*), Sri Tukaram Tatya mentions that in an ancient work called *"Saivagama"*, Lord Siva, the First Lord of Yoga urges even the perfect Yogi to persevere in his practice of Asanas and Pranayama. The scriptures also affirm that a healthy body is essential to the attainment of the goal of human existence.

It is, therefore, imperative that an aspirant who wishes to follow the path of classical Yoga should start his practices with the purification of the body, maintain it by a balanced diet and regular eating, strengthen it by proper Yogasanas and purify the nervous system by regulated breathing to help control the vagaries of the mind. Even when one is following the path of Raja Yoga, one cannot afford to ignore these practices.

I hope that this book, which is mainly based on personal experience, will be of some help to Yoga aspirants who are seeking Truth and wish to tread the path systematically.

May Lord Siva bless the seekers
after Truth with wisdom to under-
stand the science of Yoga and
strength to follow it

OM   SHANTI SHANTI SHANTI   OM